FX4
BLACK CAB

1958 to 1997 (Austin FX4, FL2; Carbodies FX4, FL2, FX4R, FX4S, FX4S-Plus, Fairway, Fairway Driver)

First published in April 2012

Bill Munro has asserted his moral right to be identified as the author of this work.

A catalogue record for this book is available from the British Library.

ISBN 978 0 85733 126 7

Library of Congress control no. 2011943849

Published by Haynes Publishing,
Sparkford, Yeovil, Somerset BA22 7JJ, UK
Tel: 01963 442030 Fax: 01963 440001
Int. tel: +44 1963 442030 Int. fax: +44 1963 440001
E-mail: sales@haynes.co.uk
Website: www.haynes.co.uk

Haynes North America Inc.
861 Lawrence Drive, Newbury Park, California 91320, USA

Printed in the USA by Odcombe Press LP,
1299 Bridgestone Parkway, La Vergne, TN 37086

COVER CUTAWAY *John Lawson*

FX4
BLACK CAB

1958 to 1997 (Austin FX4, FL2; Carbodies FX4, FL2, FX4R, FX4S, FX4S-Plus, Fairway, Fairway Driver)

Enthusiasts' Manual

An insight into the history and development
of the famous London taxi

Bill Munro

OPPOSITE **A Fairway at Victoria station, London.** *(Author)*

RIGHT **The FX4S-Plus in the finishing shop at Carbodies' factory in Coventry.** *(London Taxi Company/Taxi Newspaper Archive)*

Contents

Introduction

It is hard to think of a more instantly recognisable motor vehicle, British or otherwise, than the FX4 London taxi. First seen on the capital's streets in 1958, it has served London and many other towns and cities in the UK for over five decades, yet, if it was not for the troubles that hit the British motor industry during the 1960s and 1970s, the FX4 would surely have been replaced by a succession of more modern cabs. Instead, it survived through the sheer necessity of keeping it in production, to become an icon, not only of London, but of Britain too.

LEFT Two icons of London's transport in the late twentieth century, the Routemaster bus and the FX4 taxi. *(Barney Sharratt)*

ABOVE A London icon alongside a London landmark; a Fairway Driver passing Charing Cross. *(Barney Sharratt)*

OPPOSITE Like the Routemaster bus, the Austin FX4 was kept in service long after it was supposed to have been replaced. At the time this picture was taken in the late 1970s, the FX4 was the only cab available to the London cab trade. *(London Vintage Taxi Association Archive)*

In 1994, at a gathering of the Worshipful Company of Hackney Carriage Drivers, a good-natured confrontation was taking place. It was between Fred Housego, BBC TV *Mastermind* winner, broadcaster and cab driver extraordinaire, and Peter Wildgoose, then the sales and marketing director of London Taxis International (LTI). In a jokingly provocative way, Fred was berating Peter about the fact that the poor cabman had had to suffer the FX4 for so long.

"When", Fred asked Peter, "are we going to get a new cab? We've had to put up with exactly the same piece of junk for the past 35 years!"

Peter, delightfully urbane and unruffled as ever, couldn't give away the fact the LTI was already working on what would become the FX4's replacement, the TX1, and returned Fred's question with the skill appropriate to his talents as a tennis player.

"Fred", he said, "I can assure you that it most certainly is not the same. Virtually nothing that was on the original model back in 1958 would fit a Fairway today."

"What's new, Peter?" said Fred, looking his adversary straight in the eye, "Nothing bleedin' well fitted back then!"

Fred had a point; the build quality of the early cabs was pretty dire, but Peter was right as well. There are hardly any parts on the last Fairway model that rolled off the tracks at Coventry in the summer of 1997 that you would find exactly the same, let alone be able to fit, on the original 1958 model. The roof pressings, the interior front door handles, the door and side window glass and the interior courtesy lights are the same, and that's almost it. All the body panels have been altered in some degree, all the mechanical components, almost all the lights and other electrical items have been changed, often several times; the interior trim

has been completely redesigned. The list goes on and on.

And yet, it still looks the same, still does the same job and is still as straightforward to repair as it was in the 1960s. The fundamental concept of the cab, and its means of construction have stayed the same for all that time, and that has been its strength throughout all the troubled times of the nation and the cab trade. Its serviceability and durability has seen it and the trade through, when all attempts over the decades to find a replacement have foundered.

The Austin FX4 was designed and built with one task in mind, to operate as a purpose-built taxi in London, surely the toughest job for any urban motor vehicle, as well as complying with one unique set of rules, the Conditions of Fitness, laid down by the Metropolitan Police Public Carriage Office (PCO). The PCO had been formed a short while after the Metropolitan Police took control of London's cabs and the few remaining hackney coaches, heavy two-horse relics from the previous two centuries.

They established a firm grip on the trade and gradually brought the roguish hackney coachmen and the early cabmen who followed them into line, by introducing driver licensing and the famous 'Knowledge of London', the topographical test that every aspiring cab driver must undergo, and a driving test. They also ensured that the cabs themselves were kept up to scratch, with poorly maintained vehicles being removed from the streets.

When motor cabs first appeared, the Public Carriage Office, issued the 'Metropolitan Police Regulations for the Construction and Licensing of Hackney (Motor) Carriages, 1906'. This name was soon abbreviated to 'The Conditions of Fitness', and although these rules have been steadily updated over more than a century, two principles still apply. One is that there must be a division between driver and passengers, and the other, the famous tight-turning circle.

Thus these two rules have dictated the shape and format of the London taxi and, very soon after its introduction, consigned it to being a

BELOW This 1971 Austin was pictured at a cab trade demonstration in Lower Regent Street. *(Mal Smith Collection)*

specialist market. It is a market open to any maker. There is not a single contract awarded to any one company to build the 'London taxi', and there have been, unbelievably, close to 70 different builders who have tried their hand. Most of those appeared – and often disappeared just as quickly – before the Great War, leaving at best, a handful of manufacturers and dealers and, at times, just one of each.

Of those organisations, the most prominent and influential has been the dealership of Mann & Overton, who commissioned the FX4 from Austin. 'M&O', as they have always been known, was formed by John Mann and Tom Overton in 1897 and became involved in selling motor cabs in 1905. The company continued to trade under that name until late 2010, when it was discontinued. Now, all UK dealerships for LTI vehicles are owned and run by the renamed London Taxi Company.

Mann & Overton's dedication to the London cab trade meant that between 1973 and 1987 the already-outdated FX4 was the only model of cab available to the London market. Literally, no other company could afford to produce a cab to rival it; certainly not without the kind of subsidy that Austin provided for years out of its advertising budget. So this venerable workhorse lasted, not because it was such an exceptionally fine example of motor engineering (although it certainly had proved its fitness for the job), but because nobody responsible for it could find the money to replace it, and no other maker wanted to get involved in such a small market.

However, had the FX4 not been so durable and so serviceable, and had Mann & Overton not provided the spares and service vital for the trade, it would not have survived beyond its first few years. Even in the early years there were doubts that it would survive for long, because early models proved so troublesome, but the people behind it persevered with their investment and made it, if not perfect, then as good as they could from the resources available. Some of these improvements included better rustproofing, soundproofing and smarter interior trim, but because it was a limited production vehicle, the makers had to use as many bought-in parts as possible to keep the cost down. Many of the changes were brought about because of amendments

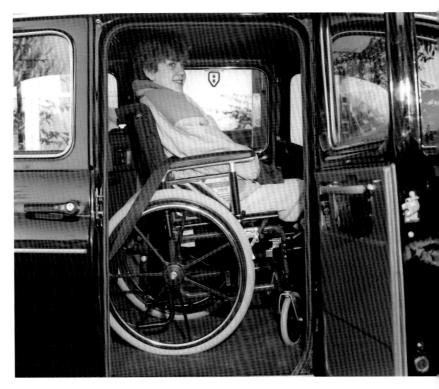

in legislation, and simply because the suppliers stopped making that particular item.

There were no more obvious examples of these enforced changes than in the types of engine fitted. A 2.5-litre diesel appeared in 1971, but this was because of British Leyland's introduction of a new medium-sized van, rather than Mann & Overton's request for improved performance, which it delivered, but the underpowered and unreliable Land Rover diesel in the FX4R turned out to be a disaster.

One of the mandatory changes, wheelchair accessibility has allowed London-type taxis, the FX4 included, to provide transport on demand to those who previously either had to plan every journey like a military operation, or else stay at home. These changes, introduced on the Fairway in 1989, were made through adaptation rather than by building them in from new, but still allowed the cab to retain its shape unaltered, and its essential versatility. Wheelchair conversions on taxis based on saloon cars have turned out, in many instances, to be monstrous, unsociable vehicles, with the person in the wheelchair isolated from their friends or family. In a London taxi, the disabled passenger is where they belong, with their travelling companions.

The Fairway, at long last, was the vehicle its makers, LTI, could export with confidence. The

ABOVE The Fairway was the first cab from LTI to provide safe transport for wheelchair-bound passengers as standard. (London Taxi Company)

style of the FX4 has, at the demand of overseas customers, been adapted for its replacement the TX1, so recognisable was it internationally. So a design that was intended to last for just ten years, has remained in its original form for 39 years, and in its modern form, well into the second decade of the 21st century.

Note: Reference to the 'nearside' and 'offside' is for the UK, i.e. on the left and right of the vehicle respectively, when looking forward.

OPPOSITE The most successful version of the FX4 at home and abroad was the Fairway. This petrol engine model was sold to an operator in Kenya. *(Stanley Roth Collection)*

BELOW The London cab trade has long supported charities, and regularly takes groups on days out. This particular event took children to Chessington World of Adventures. The cab, a Fairway Driver, was fitted with a spark-ignition engine, converted to LPG. *(Mark Cooper)*

Author's acknowledgements

I would like to thank the following people for their help in producing this book and, where appropriate, for their permission to use their photographs and images. All reasonable efforts have been made to secure permissions for image use, but if I have inadvertently missed anyone then please accept my apologies.

Peter Birch, Steve Birchall, Ross Campbell, Dave Cooper, Mark Cooper, Jery Craig, Stephen Dimmock, Hans Dooren, Timon and Jan Dyk, Roy Ellis, David Riley of Chris Hodge Trucks, Kelvin Fielding and http://SnapdragonFamilyPhotography.co.uk, Al Fresco, Chris Forteath, Mayor's Press Office, Greater London Authority and James O. Jenkins, Andrew Hall, Ivar Hellberg, Olivier Hyafil, Imperial War Museum, Murray Jackson, Robert Jankel Associates, Graham Waite, The London Vintage Taxi Association, The National Motor Museum, Andrew Overton, Stanley Roth, Barney Sharratt, Stuart Pessok, *Taxi* Newspaper, Bill Powell, Dean Reader and Sandra Mitchell of the Classic Hearse Register, Doug Scott, Don Smith, Mal Smith, Danny Stephens, Steve Tillyer, and Jimmy and Barbara Waters.

Chapter One

The FX4 story

For more than five decades, the Austin FX4, the classic 'black cab' has served both the capital and many other major cities in the UK and, towards the end of its production life, many other smaller towns too. It is known the world over as an icon of both London and Britain as a whole, but its story, one of service from the cab itself and struggle from those who built it, is far less well known.

RIGHT Victoria station, 1991. Austin FX4, VYY 41S was already fourteen years old, thanks to the PCO's relaxation of its ten-year age limit. Many of its contemporaries would stay in service until 1999. *(Author)*

ABOVE Tom Overton, co-founder of Mann & Overton's Garage, with J.J. Mann. After Mann's premature death, Tom's brother, Will joined the company and took over the running of it in the 1920s.
(Author's Collection)

The FX4's 39-year production life puts it in the same league as the Mini, the Land Rover and the Morgan, as one of the longest-running British motor vehicles of all time. As an icon of London, it is as instantly recognisable as any of these other vehicles; maybe even more so.

For the first 24 years of its life, the FX4 carried an Austin badge. It was the third successive generation of London cab to do so, but it wasn't Austin's idea to make taxis for London at all. In the late 1920s, London taxicab dealers, Mann & Overton were looking for a replacement for the revered but now obsolescent and expensive Unic they had sold since 1908. They had been selling the Austin 12/4 to the cab trade in Manchester and it had proved cheap to buy, durable and economical. In its standard production form, it would not comply with the Conditions of Fitness, the rules for London's taxi as laid down by the licensing authority, the Public Carriage Office (PCO). The car could not be modified to meet these conditions because its ground clearance was too low to meet the specified 10in minimum. This rule was changed in 1928 to allow a lower ground clearance of 7in, but the 12/4's steering and brakes had to be changed to meet the regulations that remained in place. Introduced in 1929, the Austin 12/4 taxi

became an immediate success and established Mann & Overton as the premier taxi dealer in London, a position they have never lost.

The Austin FX3

Wartime ended production of the 12/4, but in 1945, Austin produced a new taxi chassis for Mann & Overton. It was not as good as its predecessor, and after two revisions of its design, the new chassis, named the FX3, was approved by the PCO in 1948. Before the project could continue, there was a major problem to overcome, that of finding someone to make the body. Austin had never made bodies for the taxi version of the 12/4, obliging Mann & Overton to subcontract the job to several coachbuilders. Now, in the austere 1940s, coachbuilt bodies were an expensive luxury, if the timber for the frames and the craftsmen to make them could be found. An all-steel body was the thing to have, but tooling up to produce one was too expensive for Austin, to be viable for a low-volume vehicle like the taxi. Also, Austin needed all their body-making capacity to produce cars for the export drive which was vital to pull Britain from near-bankruptcy that was the result of the Second World War. They did, however, know a company that could help out.

During the Second World War, Austin had, like all British motor companies, made a major contribution to the war effort. Even before the USA entered the war, they had sent, under the Lend-Lease scheme military equipment to Britain. Large amounts of production machinery were also shipped, enabling as many spare parts for that equipment to be made in Britain as possible. Austin was asked to make fuselage panels for American aircraft, and subcontracted a Coventry coachbuilder, Carbodies Ltd, to make them, using a revolutionary material called Kirksite. Press tools could be made from this at a much lower price than if they were made from the usual material, cast steel.

Mann & Overton's Chairman, Robert Overton, met up with Carbodies' Managing Director, Ernest Jones and, with Austin, thrashed out a deal to make the FX3. It would be funded three ways, with Mann & Overton providing half the capital and Carbodies and Austin finding one-quarter each. The deal was

LEFT Although not the first cab to be sold by Mann & Overton's Garage, the 12/16 Unic was the most influential in establishing the company as London's premier taxi dealership. *(London Vintage Taxi Association Archive)*

BELOW The Austin 12/4 cab became the most numerous model in London. This is the first type, the HL, with a body by Jones Brothers of Westbourne Grove, London. *(Author)*

ABOVE More than 7,000 Austin FX3s were sold in London during the late 1940s and 1950s. With its diesel engine and black paint it established the tradition of the London 'black cab' that exists today. *(Author)*

BELOW The FL1 Hire Car provided a new vehicle for the hire car trade that would otherwise have used expensive-to-run pre-war Rolls-Royces and Daimlers. *(London Taxi Company/Barney Sharratt)*

that Austin would supply the running chassis, Carbodies build the body, mount it on the chassis, paint it, trim it and deliver it to Mann & Overton in London, who would have the sole concession for the capital. Provincial sales were to be handled by Austin themselves.

The Austin Metropolitan Taxi, to give the FX3 its full name, was an old-fashioned vehicle, styled like Austin's immediately pre-war cars, with running boards and, like the models made in the preceding decade, would have three doors and an open luggage platform beside the driver. There would also be a four-door hire car version, the FL1, with a bench front seat and, of necessity, a column gearchange and umbrella-type handbrake lever.

From the outset, the FX3 earned a good reputation for reliability, but a poor one for fuel economy. Its 2-litre petrol engine, taken from the Austin 16hp, was outrageously thirsty – 18mpg on average – and this, along with the double purchase tax levied in 1940 on cars and cabs alike, made it too expensive both to buy and to run. Doubling that tax after the Second World War made the FX3, and its competitor, the Nuffield Oxford, almost prohibitively expensive. In fact, because of the FX3's fuel consumption, every taxi proprietor in London lost money running them in the early days. Although the only other cab on the market, the Nuffield Oxford, was more economical to run, it was as expensive to buy and was discontinued in 1953 when Austin and Morris combined to form the British Motor Corporation. In these circumstances, cab proprietors hung on to their pre-war cabs rather than buy new FX3s.

Diesel power

Then, two things happened. North London taxi fleet proprietor John Birch discovered the new diesel engine that the Standard Motor Company had begun putting in the Ferguson tractor they were making, and decided to have it adapted for use in the FX3. It halved the cab's fuel consumption and fleet proprietors rushed to have Birch convert their cabs. A further benefit was that the new Conservative government, under pressure from the trade and the newly released Runciman Report on the state of the London cab trade, removed purchase tax from cabs. At last, the cab trade could operate new cabs at a profit, and sales of the FX3 took off once more.

Naturally, Austin was not happy that Birch was taking out a new, perfectly good petrol engine and installing another maker's diesel, so they developed a 2.2-litre diesel of their own from the petrol engine, and put it in the FX3. This new model, the FX3D soon became the most popular version, and reinforced Mann & Overton's position as the prominent taxi dealer in London. Not that there was any opposition to speak of then, but M&O understood the taxi business – they had been in it since 1905 – and knew that prompt, even instant economical servicing and totally reliable cabs were essential to keep the trade viable.

The FX4 – design and development

As the FX3 approached its sixth birthday, Mann & Overton put plans in hand to replace it with a new model, and again they spoke to Austin, who had served them well since 1929, and to Carbodies, who had done a first-class job of building the cab. There had been a lot of changes at both Austin and Carbodies since the FX3 first appeared. Austin was now part of the British Motor Corporation and Carbodies' owner, Bobby Jones, had sold out in 1954 to BSA, who put it under the wing of one of its constituent companies, Daimler.

At this time, the BSA empire was run by Sir Bernard Docker and his flamboyant wife, Lady Nora Docker. There were many stories about Lady Docker in the press of the day, especially about how she spent huge amounts of company money on one-off extravagant, coachbuilt Daimlers such as the Golden Zebra, a 20ft-long coupé with gold-plated trim, ivory dashboard and real zebra skin upholstery. Equally, there were many tales within the BSA companies related to her extravagance, none more relevant to our story than when the BSA board opted to buy the most up-to-date and expensive plant and machinery for their factories, before her ladyship got her hands on the cash! Carbodies benefited from this strategy when several large, high-quality presses were delivered to their factory in Holyhead Road. This outlay, along with investment in cast-steel

press tools would help keep the costs of the next model of taxi down and do away with Carbodies' reliance on the softer, less durable Kirksite to produce the body panels.

According to new practice, the initial design of the new cab was given the Austin code of ADO6 (standing for Austin Drawing Office, project No. 6), but the design staff soon reverted to the old Austin system, and renumbered it as the FX4. Austin's chief stylist, Ricardo 'Dick' Burzi, was busy on two other projects, the Metropolitan and the Farina A40, so his chief design engineer, Jim Stanfield, gave the job of designing the new taxi to a relative junior, Eric Bailey. Bailey was delighted to be given the assignment and approached it with some humility, realising that, while the new cars that were being designed in the same building would have very sharp styling by the Italian house of Pininfarina, the new cab would be much more utilitarian. It would also have a working life of around ten years, so should not look dated. Drawing on his work with the Sheerline and the A30, he produced, in his own words "… a pleasant shape that would not cause offence to anyone".

While Jim Stanfield kept an eye on young Bailey, the design of the chassis was left to an old hand, Phil Baker, who had worked on the FX3. He produced a conventional X-braced, channel-section design, to which Stanfield fitted the independent coil-spring front suspension designed

BELOW Photographed in 1992, Eric Bailey, the man who styled the FX4, studies his original artwork for the cab, some 36 years after he created it.
(Barney Sharratt)

for the new A99 Westminster and Wolseley 6/99 models, along with the same type of back axle. The brakes would be drum all round, with dual-circuit hydraulics, operated from master cylinders under the floorboards. The steering was a worm-and-peg design, adapted to cope with the much tighter turning circle of the taxi.

Bailey's original design for the body was a full-width one, but having three doors and an open luggage platform, like the FX3 before it. The headlights were placed inboard of the front wings, similar to the location on the Austin A30 and Princess, upon which Bailey had worked. In fact, there is a clear similarity between the lines of the A30's front wings and those of the production FX4.

A full-size mock-up was shown to Mann & Overton's Chairman, Robert Overton, and Managing Director, David Southwell, and Herbert Gould, the head of the Public Carriage Office. Gould suggested that the cab should have a fourth door, and recommended that the windscreen should be able to open, so that the cabmen could see better in the 'pea-soup' fogs that beset London in those days. He expressed a dislike for the 'crocodile' bonnet, hinged on the scuttle, which he said might fly open at speed, and blind the driver.

It may seem strange that, in the mid-1950s, when a new generation of cars like the Ford Zephyr, Humber Super Snipe and the Jaguar 3.4 litre were either new or about to be released, that Austin's drawing office should even consider such an old-fashioned design of cab as the first

three-door rendition of the FX4, let alone put it forward for approval, especially as the cars were some of the most stylish British models yet to be seen. But experienced men at 'The Austin', like Stanfield and Baker, had a track record of working with the Conditions of Fitness, the Public Carriage Office's rules for the design and construction of taxis, and knew how difficult the PCO could be when it came to new ideas.

The Public Carriage Office was not run by time-served motor engineers but by serving policemen who had been trained in motor engineering. Although they were prepared to consider innovation, their overriding brief was one of public safety and they had to take responsibility for decisions that resulted in any human casualty caused by the failure or inadequacy of any equipment fitted to a London taxicab. Thus, they often erred on the side of caution and would take far too long to be sure that what was offered was safe and feasible. The manufacturers would therefore hold back, knowing that if they presented an established or even outdated design, it would at least be accepted without too much delay, whereas the motor industry would press ahead with new designs, leaving the cab design and specification way behind.

Towards production

Gould at least was forward-looking, so Bailey took the points he made and returned with some new full-colour sketches, one picture showing a cream and white cab with a wrap-

BELOW The first sketch of the FX4, produced by Eric Bailey. The headlamps are inboard of the front wings and the bonnet is inset into the wings, as on contemporary saloon cars. The roof line and the shape of the rear window would remain almost unchanged.
(Author's Collection)

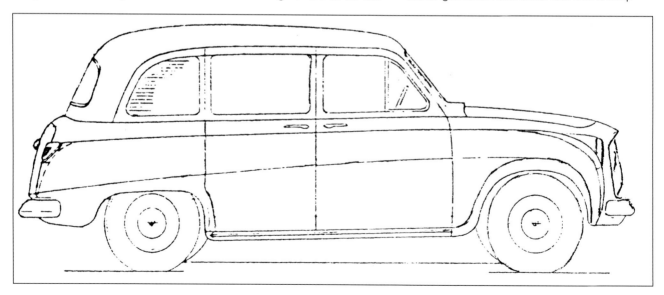

LEFT The familiar design begins to take shape. Bailey included a two-tone colour scheme, which was becoming very popular with motor manufacturers. The front wing line was changed with the headlamps mounted on the centreline. The 'set-in' bonnet design of the first sketch has given way to one with the grille built in.

LEFT Another two-tone scheme. New technology within the glass industry enabled wrap-around windows to be made and these, like the two-tone, pastel paint, were gaining favour with some makers. BMC, however, would never use such extreme curvature on any of the glass in its private cars.

LEFT The final design, approved by Robert Overton, and very close to the production models.
(All courtesy Barney Sharratt)

around rear window. Robert Overton took a liking to another sketch in the collection, of a red and cream cab with a simple curved rear window and distinctive swage lines. The next step was to develop the basic idea into a full workable design, and then send the drawings to Carbodies, for their chief design engineer, Jake Donaldson, to produce detail drawings of all the many different body parts, and prepare it for production.

Although Donaldson had not worked on the design of the FX3, his former boss, chief draughtsman Don Cobb, had, and taught him well about the cab trade's needs. Donaldson designed the body to have fully unboltable sills and wings, to make repairs quick and economical. The interior panels were each made of a single plastic moulding for easy cleaning and durability, and the floor mat was rubber to enable it to be washed easily. Like the front suspension, brakes and most of the steering parts, the rest of the mechanical components were standard items found on medium to large BMC cars, which kept the production costs down and made servicing straightforward. The proven 2.2-litre diesel

engine from the FX3 was carried over, but the only transmission offered at first was a Borg-Warner DG150M automatic. This was because the cab proprietors demanded an automatic transmission. Older cab drivers had spent years driving cabs with crash gearboxes and, rather than change down in traffic, would slip the clutch, thus creating far greater wear than was economical. The Borg-Warner DG150M had been tested in a small number of FX3s, and had shown to be reliable, so it was adopted for the FX4.

The FX4 was the first production London taxi to feature independent front suspension and four full doors. Hydraulic brakes were fitted to the Beardmore Mk7, which had been approved in 1954 and also on the Birch prototype, which also had independent front suspension. The reasons why these features were so late in appearing in London taxis, or more specifically an Austin taxi, are twofold. One is that London taxis have, since the 1930s, been built for a service life of ten years. This meant that its specification would inevitably become obsolete during the production run. It also meant that any advances in vehicle technology would not be

BELOW Jack Hellberg, seen here climbing out of the pre-production FX4, VLW 431, at BSA's head office was Carbodies director and general manager at the time of the cab's development and launch. Very popular with the staff at the factory, he always wore a bow tie and a fresh flower in his buttonhole.
(Ivar Hellberg)

adopted until the time was right for a new cab to be designed. The effect of this protracted service life was greatly affected by the timing of the arrival of the FX4's predecessor, the FX3.

Huge technological advances had been made during the Second World War, but car design development had, officially, been frozen for the duration. The new cars that appeared on the market in late 1945 were either based on pre-war models or were those actual pre-war models, pushed back into production to meet the demand. Although car makers, during the time they were producing war material, were planning and dreaming about what they would produce, they were forbidden to actually make those dreams reality until the end of hostilities. It would take several years before any truly new models would appear. In Austin's case, the first all-new private cars, the A40 Devon and the Princess and Sheerline, were launched at the 1947 Motor Show.

Nevertheless, there was a demand for new taxis in London after the end of the war, as all pre-war models had been taken out of production. To ensure that Austin were able to supply the chassis for one, they built it using what they had to hand. For Austin, this meant mechanical brakes, because they had not embraced hydraulic braking systems like some of their rivals, and beam axles with leaf springs, for the same reason. It also meant using a design of body that was of pre-war style, although the landaulette hood, favoured so much by proprietors, would be banned by the PCO because they wanted cabs to be more like modern cars in appearance, while maintaining a distinct appearance. Thus the Austin FX4 was the first truly 'modern' London taxi in all respects that would go into production.

Into service

Production problems

The first model off the production lines, VLW 431, went on trial in the summer of 1958 with a trusted proprietor, York Way Motors, and attracted a lot of attention. A Hire Car version, the FL2, would also be made, to sell to the private hire and funeral trades. The FL2 was introduced at the Earls Court Motor Show, while the taxi made its formal debut at the same

BELOW The first pre-production FX4, VLW 431 photographed by the gates of South Park, Fulham, not far from Mann & Overton's premises. This cab featured in promotional films and went on test with fleet proprietors York Way Motors in King's Cross. *(Author's Collection)*

ABOVE Carbodies always occupied the same spot at the Commercial Motor Exhibition at Earls Court, beside the escalator. This was their 1960 offering. The cab retained the original door handles, but the aperture in the partition had been changed. *(Chris Hodge Trucks)*

RIGHT The FL2 Hire Car on Carbodies' stand at the Motor Show, Earls Court in 1958. Note the absence of a roof sign. Alongside it are Ford Consul, Zephyr and Zodiac convertibles, which were also produced by Carbodies. *(Chris Hodge Trucks)*

time at the Commercial Motor Exhibition and went on sale soon after, at a price of just under £1,200. However, when Carbodies tried to put the cab into production, the real trouble started. The press tools were of very bad quality, especially for the roof and the bonnet, and in the first full year of production just 216 cabs actually found their way to customers. To help resolve the situation, Carbodies' management called in a former employee of the company, toolmaker Bill Lucas, to sort things out. Lucas altered a lot of the tooling and ordered new tools for the roof and the boot, which finally got the cab into full production. He rejoined the company and would go on to become managing director.

The automatic gearbox, a thing the proprietors were looking forward to, caused a lot of trouble and made them wish they never asked for it. For one thing, it was a total mismatch for the engine and, also, older cabmen did not have a clue how to use one. Often, they would put the engine into neutral at traffic lights, then rev the engine and slam the 'box into gear, causing internal damage as the engine tried to turn the gears against the resistance of the brakes. Eventually, in 1961, the manual gearbox from the contemporary Austin

ABOVE An early FX4, photographed in the yard of Carbodies' factory in Coventry. The straight door handles proved too fragile in use. *(NMM)*

BELOW Although the London General Cab Company was critical of the FX4 at its introduction, it had no choice but to buy them, gradually replacing their fleet of Austin FX3s. Both models can be seen here in one of the mechanical workshops in the mid-1960s. *(Mal Smith Collection)*

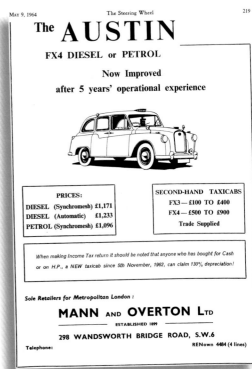

ABOVE The licence granted to a London taxi by the Public Carriage Office (now Transport for London, Taxis and Private Hire) lasts for a calendar year. Before inspection for that licence, each cab has to be overhauled and part of the process is a steam clean and chassis paint. This is the London General's own steam cleaning section. *(Mal Smith Collection)*

BELOW Although mechanically the FL2 Hire Car was virtually the same as the FX4 taxi, it differed externally and internally. Missing from the FL2 was the roof sign, and the limpet indicators were dropped around 1962. *(Author)*

ABOVE The wording of this advertisement shows tacit acceptance from M&O that the FX4 needed improvement. They appear to be selling second-hand FX3s, the newest of which were then only six years old. In fact, they offered introductions to buyers and sellers of used cabs and provided owner-to-owner finance, rather than buying in cabs and selling them on. *(London Vintage Taxi Association Archive)*

Gypsy was fitted. In 1962, a petrol engine was offered and in 1964, the unsuitable DG150M auto 'box was replaced with the new BW35.

Export attempts

Austin had sold the FX3 to export markets with varying, but ultimately unstained success, including a left-hand drive three-door model to Canada, and four-door versions to the USA, which were a failure, and 500 to Madrid in Spain. The first attempt to sell the FX4 abroad was in 1960, to New York City, but this again proved a failure. There was only a diesel version available and petrol was so cheap in the USA that no operator wanted to lay out the high cost for what was an already antiquated and expensive vehicle. It was too cold in the winter, too hot in the summer, too slow, too noisy and shook itself to bits on the potholes that peppered the roads of 'The Big Apple'.

The next export attempt came in late 1967 as a result of an initiative by the then mayor of New York City, John V. Lindsay. Lindsay was a tall man and had trouble getting in and out of the sedan cabs operated in his city and wanted purpose-built cabs, that had been required by city regulations until a few years before. Austin prepared a special left-hand drive version, developed from the FL2 Hire Car, using that model's forward-facing tip-up seats and a unique combination of the 2.2-litre petrol engine and an automatic gearbox. The cab, along with a taxi version of the Peugeot 404, went on trial in the summer of 1968. Both were a failure. Competition for the American taxi market was fierce, and US car dealers would offer special deals that undercut the proposed $3,500 price of the FX4 by close on $1,000. Besides, the FX4, with a sluggish four-cylinder engine and no optional air conditioning or power steering was hopelessly outclassed by contemporary American models. The project never got off the ground, and it would be over a decade before the American market was considered again.

RIGHT Graham Whitehead, president of British Motor Holdings (USA) presented the special New York City version of the FX4 to the city's Mayor, John V. Lindsay. (Steering Wheel Publications/ Stanley Roth Collection)

12   The Steering Wheel   JUNE 29, 1968

THE SEARCH FOR AN IDEAL CAB

OR HOW THE FX4 WENT TO NEW YORK

Austin Taxi in the driveway of Gracie Mansion, official home of New York City's mayors, prior to the presentation to Mayor John V. Lindsay.

photo by British Motor Holdings (U.S.A.) Inc.

Whether Mayor John Lindsay thinks he has found the perfect cab for the streets of New York in the Austin FX4, is open to divergent opinion.

The Steering Wheel conducted its own enquiries to answer these questions: Briefly we set out to discover how and by what means the 'London Cab in New York' experiment was initiated. For what reasons? How is the cab specifically being used? And, what is the reaction of the Manhattan taxi drivers, New York trade officials, and the Mayor, himself, to the London cab which is now in New York?

Mayor Lindsay started his search for the ideal cab after a lifetime of struggling to squeeze his 6 ft. 4 ins. frame into the cramped rear of New York's present cabs. Late last year the Mayor delivered a speech calling for a more compact, yet spacious cab which was "quieter, smaller, neater . . ." to replace (to what extent we *don't* know) some of the Dodges, Fords, and Chevrolet cabs in the city.

From Mr. Graham Whitehead, President of British Motor Holdings (U.S.A.) Inc., *The Steering Wheel* received the following letter:

Dear Sir,

Following a speech by Mayor Lindsay of New York late last year regarding the unsuitability of Detroit automobiles for taxi work and praising foreign built cabs, I offered the Mayor the use of an Austin FX4 taxi for extended testing by the City. The offer was accepted and the Mayor also asked a number of other overseas taxi manufacturers to participate.

We immediately arranged for a cab to be shipped on the "S.S. Scythia". The unit has automatic gear box, petrol engine and is painted bright yellow. The rear jump seats have been modified to face forward to conform to the New York City Hack Bureau requirements. The Austin was officially handed over to Mayor Lindsay at his Gracie Mansion residence on May 14th, and the only other foreign cab that was present was a small Peugeot. It is intended that the Austin will be allocated to a cab company who will put it into regular service on July 1st and will be operated by their usual drivers.

JUNE 29, 1968   The Steering Wheel   13

It is too early yet to have any reaction of New York taxi drivers and union officials, and the few I have spoken to so far seem to have mixed feelings.

Yours sincerely,
G. W. Whitehead,
President.

British Motor Holdings (U.S.A.) Inc.

When this offer was accepted, British Motor Corporation (Birmingham) Ltd. produced a special London taxi modified for American specifications, painted it yellow, and despatched it to Mayor Lindsay. Unlike the majority of the Austin taxis used in London, this one has a 2.2 litre petrol engine with automatic transmission and is, of course, left hand drive. The vehicle was shown by Mr. J. W. Bache, a Director of BMC Export Sales Division, to Alderman Jim Meadows, Birmingham's Lord Mayor, before starting on its journey to Liverpool and thence to New York. Along with the taxi, went a message of goodwill from the Lord Mayor to Mayor Lindsay.

On May 14th, Mayor Lindsay inspected the Austin FX4 and Peugeot 404 at his Gracie Mansion residence. Presenting the Austin to the Mayor was Graham Whitehead, President of British Motor Holdings (U.S.A.) Inc.. Henri Combe, Executive Vice President of Peugeot, Inc., presented the Peugeot 404. Attending the delivery were Jack Plotsky, President of the Metropolitan Taxicab Board of Trade; representatives of the Taxi Drivers' Union, Local 3036, AFL-CIO; and Nathan H. Karlin, President of Kay Taximeter

Company, who installed meters in both automobiles.

Predictably enough, but for understandable reasons, only limited replies to *The Steering Wheel's* enquiries could be given from the Office of the Mayor of New York and the Office of the Police Commissioner at this time.

We reprint them here:

Dear Sir,

For some time we have been looking for a comfortable, economical vehicle which would be better suited to taxi use than the present standard sedans, with their small rear compartments and overpowered engines.

We have contacted several foreign manufacturers including Austin and Peugeot, both of which have supplied us with a test vehicle.

If features of these vehicles meet with the approval of driver and public, they may eventually be incorporated in New York cabs.

Sincerely,
Dan Tessler,
Assistant to the Mayor.

Office of the Mayor of New York,
New York.

And from the Police Department of the City of New York:

Dear Sir,

There is an experiment presently being contemplated in New York City involving the use of two vehicles, the Austin and Peugeot. At this time, plans are being

continued next page

Left to Right: Dan Tessler, Assistant to the Mayor, Mayor John Lindsay and Graham W. Whitehead, President of British Motor Holdings (U.S.A.) Inc., examine the headroom of the Austin Taxi. Mayor Lindsay, who is 6' 4", commented on the ease of access.

photo by British Motor Holdings (U.S.A.) Inc.

'new shape' Austins
came out in 1969, on
a G-plate. Externally,
the differences were
in the lights, with
the hated 'limpet'
indicators consigned
to history, replaced
by tail lights from the
Austin and Morris
MkII 1100/1300 range.
The heavy rubber sill
trim can be seen. This
FX4, photographed in
Constitution Hill, by
Buckingham Palace,
belonged to the
London General
Cab Company. *(Mal
Smith Collection)*

A first try at a replacement

Back home, the cab trade finally got used
to the FX4, and hard work on the part of
Carbodies and Austin improved it, although
it was still prone to rust and the lack of
soundproofing made it a strain to drive.
However, towards the end of the 1960s the
trade anticipated a replacement model. That is
what Mann & Overton were planning, but when,
in 1966, Carbodies quoted them £350,000 for
a new body, they thought again. M&O spoke
to both Jensen and Gordon-Keeble about
having a glassfibre body designed and built.
Both were making high-quality sports saloons
with glassfibre bodies and were capable of
producing the quality needed. Certainly, Jensen
would have had the capacity to build a new cab
at a rate of 50 or more a week. However, on
the advice of Austin's Joe Edwards, who was a
specialist in body production, they abandoned
the idea.

The 'new shape'

The fact that the existing FX4 left a lot to be
desired, despite gradual improvements to
its standard of finish, was not lost on Mann
& Overton. Rather than spend a huge sum
on a completely new model, they settled on
a revision of the existing model, a 'Mark II'
version, similar to what BMC had done with
their front-wheel drive range. Known in the
trade as the 'new shape' (although it varied only
in detail from the previous model) it came out in
1969, tackling the main criticisms of the original.
The old partition with the sliding glass from the
FL2 Hire Car was redesigned, soundproofing
added and the hated roof-mounted indicators
were replaced with the rear-light clusters from
the BMC 1100/1300 MkII range. It made the
cab better to drive, and the rustproofing was
improved, but still it was the same old FX4 and
the trade wanted something new. It would have
to wait until the late 1970s for even a promise.

ABOVE A 1968 Austin FX4, photographed at a demonstration by the cab trade over the proposed imposition of VAT on cab fares. It carried a different bonnet badge from the earlier model, and the paint around the inside window frames was changed on this model from tan to body colour. *(Mal Smith Collection)*

LEFT Three men closely involved with the FX4 in its early years, and one man who would help Carbodies towards becoming a complete maker in its own right, from left to right: Bill Lucas, managing director of Carbodies Ltd, David Southwell, managing director of Mann & Overton, Robert Overton, chairman of Mann & Overton, maker and dealers respectively. Far right is George Turnbull, managing director of British Leyland's Austin-Morris division, which sold the FX4 chassis manufacturing plant to Carbodies Ltd. *(London Taxi Company)*

RIGHT The chassis of the FX4 was subject to several detail changes to comply with new EEC rules on vehicle safety. Visible here are the different steering wheel with energy-absorbing centre, and the crash link in the steering column, fitted just above the steering box. *(Mal Smith Collection)*

BELOW The most obvious external change made to the FX4 after 1974 was the push-button door handles and opening quarterlights. The plastic overriders were fitted from 1977. *(Author)*

A new engine

In the meantime, Carbodies tried their best to improve the FX4, restricted by, or on occasions helped by, regulation, and sometimes by a change in the supply of components, but always tempered by a lack of cash. The first of these improvements, resulting in a change of specification, was a bigger engine. British Leyland, the new conglomerate of British Motor Holdings and Leyland, introduced a new light van, the Austin-Morris AE350. This had a new, 2.5-litre version of the diesel engine, which was put in the FX4 from late 1971. In conjunction with a higher-ratio differential, it improved the cab's performance, boosting top speed to nearly 70mph.

More improvements

A package of changes then came about through legislation, and improved the FX4's safety in the event of a collision. From late 1971, Britain's entry into the Common Market brought new vehicle regulations, including the need for a crash test. It also imposed the requirement for burst-proof door locks, from which the FX4 had been exempt for some time. Along with these locks, push-button door handles were fitted and the internal passenger door handles were relocated to the centre of the doors. A new instrument panel was also designed and, at long last, the self-cancelling indicator switch, originally mounted in the centre of the dash, and which always ceased to work after about five years, was replaced by a stalk on the steering column. A new steering wheel was fitted, with an energy-absorbing centre boss. Although the build quality was gradually improved, the FX4 was getting further and further behind the times and the price, thanks to inflation, rose from £1,200 in 1970 to almost £7,000 in 1980.

So why wasn't there a replacement in the early 1970s, when the trade wanted one? Quite simply, at British Leyland there wasn't the money, or suitable base vehicles on which to build it. The existing chassis was up to the job. By now, the big Austin and Wolseley saloons had disappeared and the only other suspension available within British Leyland's Austin-Morris division was either the torsion-bar set up from the Marina, which was too light, and the Hydrolastic setup, which would cost a lot of money to develop and would offer no real benefit. Neither was there a better engine for the job. The computer-aided technology and advances in manufacturing that would result in the refined diesel engines we enjoy today had barely been dreamed of. The only other option was a new body, but for what? The original one was now better built and did its job well enough. So why change?

The LM11 – a lost cause from the start

There was an attempt to build an entirely new cab, the LM11, on a proposed medium-sized van, but it was a disaster. Mann & Overton, although profitable, were not willing to fund a new model, partly because they had a captive market and saw no need for one: sales were at their highest level ever, even in the slump during the early 1970s caused by the three-day week. Carbodies had problems of their own. Their owner, BSA, was in deep trouble and in 1973, the government, not wanting to see the British motorcycle industry collapse, pressured Manganese Bronze Holdings Plc (MBH), who owned Norton Motorcycles, into buying BSA. Part of MBH's restructuring was to close the modern Triumph factory at Meriden, but the unions had other ideas and, forming a cooperative, took over the factory. This action starved MBH of funds that might have improved the FX4 and provided for a new model.

Trouble for FL2 sales

One factor that affected sales of FL2 and FX4 variants was purchase tax. It had been applied to taxis after the Second World War and removed from this category in 1953. It remained applicable to private cars until replaced by Value Added Tax (VAT) and the special car tax in 1973. Only commercial vehicles and taxis were exempt from purchase tax, so until 1973, an FL2 Hire Car was subject to purchase tax, including both limousine and hearse variants, whereas a van built on an FX4 chassis was not. All motor vehicles became subject to VAT on its introduction in 1973, including London taxis and the FL2 became subject to special car tax.

The FL2 Hire Car had been updated with the same changes that were made to the taxi. Although the petrol engine option had been dropped in 1973, it had sold steadily to the provincial private hire trade, but those sales would be severely curtailed by an Act of Parliament in 1976 that allowed local government authorities to licence private hire vehicles. The use of such vehicles, widely known of course as minicabs, had grown, unrestricted for a decade and a half and a rogue element had control of a significant section of the trade, both as drivers and company operators. This caused concern among both safety campaigners and the licensed taxi trade across the country. Drivers of private hire vehicles were not, and still are not, allowed to pick up passengers in the street in the same way as licensed taxi drivers are. However, not only were minicab drivers openly plying for hire but opportunists, who were not even working for a minicab company, were operating as bogus minicabs, charging exorbitant rates and on occasions preying on lone women. After the Act was passed, pressure was put on local authorities to intervene, and most did, by licensing private hire vehicles.

As a way to self-enforce illegal plying for hire, a part of the Act specified that any vehicle that was type-approved as a taxi by the Public Carriage Office could not be licensed for private hire outside the Capital. Only one vehicle fitted this description: the FL2, and now no provincial private hire operator, law-abiding or otherwise was able to use it. Sales were restricted to those who wanted a special type of limousine, which was a very small market indeed.

Soldiering on

In the early years of the FX4's production, Carbodies' management had very little contact with Mann & Overton, the very people

responsible for the FX4's creation. There were three main areas of concern. First, Mann & Overton rarely saw a cab after it had passed out of its six-month/6,000-mile warranty, the threshold of which was usually reached in less than two months. So they were unaware of a lot of the problems that cab proprietors had to deal with as a cab got older. Secondly, as car design, and for that matter light commercial vehicle design, improved and more 'extras' were fitted, such as reversing lights and two-speed wipers, the cab trade expected to see these things fitted to the FX4.

Mann & Overton, on the other hand, would not pay for these items unless they were required by a change in the law, or the component suppliers stopped making the existing parts. Thirdly, Carbodies had always had several contracts on the go and the taxi had to share the attention of the management along with the other contacts. In the late 1940s, they had devised a method of making convertibles out of steel saloon cars and had, in the 1960s, gone over to producing estate cars for Rootes and Triumph, the latest being the Triumph 2000. This type of work was beginning to dry up as car makers took these jobs, previously considered as specialist, in-house and the taxi would soon become the company's only product, so they would soon need to increase production to keep the factory viable.

The trouble was that Mann & Overton had a two-year waiting list for new cabs, regular sales to a captive market and a monopoly by default, the result of the other makers (and there had only been two minor players, Beardmore and Winchester in the 1960s), and did not see any reason to make any changes.

Bill Lucas, who for 14 years held the top job at Carbodies, strove to bring the build quality of the FX4 to as high a level as he could, and made his job easier by establishing a working relationship with the Chief Inspecting Officer of the PCO, Jack Everitt. Through Everitt, Lucas began to understand the foibles and weaknesses of ageing FX4s and was able, given the financial restraints imposed by Mann & Overton, to improve the quality of the vehicle.

The FX5

Eventually, tired of those financial restraints Lucas decided to take matters into his own hands and put in place the FX5 project, a cab that would be free of Mann & Overton's influence. It had modern styling, the running gear from the contemporary Rover SD1 and a Peugeot engine. After a scale model had been produced and approved, a chassis was made and a mock-up of the body built and press tools for the body ordered and made. But it was not to be. Lucas suffered ill health

and retired in 1979. He was replaced by Grant Lockhart, who scrapped the FX5, choosing instead to revive an idea thought up by Jake Donaldson and discarded by him and Lucas. It was to make a new cab from a Range Rover body. It would be called the CR6.

Smartening up

Up until the late 1970s, any individual wanting to buy a new cab had to find a 25 per cent deposit. This at the time meant finding almost £2,000. Then a new way of financing cabs, lease-hire, became available. This allowed the potential buyer to take delivery of a new cab for a sum equivalent to one month's repayments, which in practice worked out at around £250. It resulted in an increase in the number of sales to individual owner drivers, and a drop in sales to fleet proprietors, who until that time had bought at least half of Mann & Overton's output. To try to generate some extra profit, a range of optional extras was offered, including a vinyl roof, a sunroof, a chrome rubbing strip, and an

additional colour, midnight blue. Personal radios had only recently been permitted by the PCO, and these could be fitted, in a roof binnacle that covered the aperture that gave access to the roof sign light. Only a single speaker was permitted, of just 4 watts, so as not to impose on the passengers' privacy.

The outgoing Labour government had engaged Michael Edwardes to thrash British Leyland into profitability and make it ready for re-privatisation, and that included restructuring Austin-Morris, the renamed division responsible for supplying the FX4's mechanical components. New European legislation was on the horizon too, demanding type approval for passenger-carrying vehicles. Austin-Morris had lost interest in the FX4, and was not willing to prepare for type approval. If this were not done, the FX4 would have to be scrapped. The CR6 was nowhere near ready for production so Lockhart took matters into his own hands, acquiring the intellectual rights for the FX4 and presenting it for approval in Carbodies' own name. From the spring of 1982, it would no longer be an Austin; it would be the Carbodies FX4.

The FX4R

Through his rationalisation programme, Edwardes dealt a second blow to Carbodies,

by selling the 2.5-litre Austin diesel to an Indian company. This was done because it would not pass new exhaust emission standards. Trials had been conducted with a new 2.5-litre Peugeot engine, which was planned for the FX5, but this engine was proving troublesome and the trials had to be abandoned. The only other engine that was available, which in any way met Carbodies' requirements, was the 2.3-litre Land Rover. It seemed to be an ideal engine, being about the same physical size, only slightly smaller in capacity and producing the same horsepower, and when Carbodies' engineers installed it, it seemed to fit and run nicely.

Two innovations long overdue on the FX4 were fitted to the FX4R. These were power steering, originally as an option, and full-servo brakes, controlled by a new pendant pedal setup. The Land Rover engine was also made in a petrol version and, the diesel being a direct conversion of it, was physically identical, so would fit with no modifications apart from a different fuel supply system and minor adaptations of the driver's controls. Thus Grant Lockhart, seeing a further marketing outlet in the provinces and overseas decided to offer a petrol version and also revamp the FL2 Hire Car. Rebranded as the London Limousine, it would have the option of either petrol or diesel engine. The trim options, with choices of vinyl roof, sunroof, different colours and a rubbing strip along the front wings and front doors available on the FX4D, were carried over to the FX4R, but offered as three separate packages: FL (Fleetline), HL (Highline), and HLS (Highline Special). Prices were higher, not only to recoup the development costs of the new model but Carbodies was a stand-alone company, without the backing of Austin. The cost of an FX4R ranged from the FL with a manual gearbox at £8,869.25, to £10,071.70 for an HLS automatic.

However, the timescale for all these developments was a mere three months, which was an impossibly short time. The upshot was that FX4R turned out to be a disaster and, from its introduction in late 1982, gave no end of trouble. Quite simply, the engine had too little torque, a weak valve train and, thanks to a poorly designed combustion chamber, it smoked excessively. Its performance and its fuel consumption were well below what was expected. A regularly heard story from

RIGHT From the very first, the basic method of building an FX4 never varied. The body was built up, minus the front wings and bonnet, and lowered on to the chassis. This is an FX4R automatic receiving its body. The brake master cylinder and reservoir was mounted in front of the servo, and the rectangular metal structure carried both it and the pedal assembly. *(London Vintage Taxi Association Archive)*

embarrassed and infuriated cab drivers was that they could not drive up Highgate Hill, arguably the steepest, longest hill in Greater London, with four passengers and luggage. Other problems involved a faulty installation of the optional five-speed manual Rover gearbox, which caused the gearbox to self-destruct. It was with the FX4R that Carbodies hoped to move into new markets in the UK and abroad, but it nearly brought the company to its knees and gave it a poor reputation in markets outside London that would take a decade or more to live down.

Alternative engines

The FX4R's poor acceleration and hill-climbing ability prompted some companies to offer replacement engines. The most popular was the 3-litre Perkins, available from TLS and fitted by Motor & Diesel of Cambridgeshire. Other options included a 3.5-litre Mazda (which was in reality a larger version of the Perkins), although it is not known if any were fitted and, later, a 2.5-litre Nissan. The London Cab Company (formerly the London General Cab Company) offered a 2.5-litre conversion for the Land Rover, using a longer-throw crankshaft, which gave greater torque and thus better pulling power.

In 1986, the London Cab Company fitted a number of their FX4Rs with Ford FSD diesel engines, the same type as used in the Transit, mated to the existing automatic gearboxes. East London cab proprietors Nelson Crouch bought some, but by 1987 they were selling them off. The Ford engine was a reliable unit, and gave long life, but it was much noisier than the Land Rover or the Perkins. All of these made the FX4R a lot easier to drive, even though it did nothing to address the squeaks, rattles and leaks that had kept cabmen company for the previous two decades.

LEFT Perkins Vehicle Power is what the advert says, and power is what it gave the FX4R, in abundance. *(London Vintage Taxi Association Archive)*

Export attempts

Even more problems arose in the export markets, especially to the Middle East. Such an iconic vehicle had to be offered abroad, and was to several Middle Eastern states, such as Saudi Arabia and Dubai. It was offered, variously as either a taxi or a limousine, mostly with a petrol engine, depending on the laws and requirements of the country into which they were imported. But in comparison with such well-established brands as Mercedes-Benz, the FX4R was hopelessly outclassed and the engine was nowhere near capable of handling the power-sapping air-conditioning system vital in these countries. Its much more intense servicing schedule was not appreciated by the people charged with dealing with them. Again, the cab was a failure, and an expensive one at that. A huge amount of development money was spent in return for major losses.

CR6 troubles

To make matters worse for Carbodies, the CR6 was devouring development money at a colossal rate. Its progress had been on schedule until the Department of Transport asked if a London taxi could be adapted to take a wheelchair-bound passenger. Seeing that this would be a worthwhile benefit, Lockhart had both CR6 prototypes adapted to take a wheelchair. Trials took place outside London, but the timing of them set the schedule back almost two years and devoured even more money. Eventually, Manganese Bronze pulled the plug on the CR6 and continued to make the FX4.

THE FX4Q

A curious version of the FX4 was the FX4Q. These were actually complete rebuilds of older Austin cabs. They were introduced by Grant Lockhart as a way of keeping production lines

BELOW The FX4Q was almost indistinguishable from the Austin or Carbodies FX4. *(Stephen Dimmock)*

busy as sales of the FX4R slumped. The company took an old chassis, stripped it, renovated it and fitted fully reconditioned suspension and axles (later, new parts) and installed the Indian-made version of the original 2.5-litre Austin diesel. This could be used because the donor vehicle was built before the introduction of the emission standard that had resulted in the disposal of the Austin engine. The FX4Q was fitted with the FX4R's full servo-braking system and an automatic gearbox as standard, but not with power steering. It would be sold by Rebuilt Taxicabs Ltd, a division of a London cab fleet proprietor at a lower price than the FX4R. Mann & Overton were appalled at the decision, justifiably maintaining that Carbodies was undercutting its own sales. Unfortunately for Carbodies, and fortunately for Mann & Overton, the FX4Q was unreliable, and earned a poor reputation.

London Taxis International and the FX4S

New management at Carbodies

Carbodies was dispirited by the failure of the FX4R and other aborted projects, but a new managing director, Barry Widdowson, began to bring the company up to scratch and improve the FX4. To bring everything together, Manganese Bronze Holdings bought Mann & Overton from the company that had owned it for almost a decade, Lloyds Bowmaker. Now, all decision making about the FX4 and any successive models would be made in-house, removing any external conflict. Carbodies, Mann & Overton and M&O's own finance house were renamed and reformed as three separate divisions: LTI Carbodies, to make the cabs, LTI Mann & Overton to sell them, and London Taxi Finance to provide money to the trade, both fleet proprietors and owner-drivers.

Land Rover had been developing a new 2.5-litre diesel engine and it was hoped that this could have been fitted from the outset, but it was not ready by the time the FX4R's design work was under way. Examples were put on test in 1983, and in early 1985 a revised model with the larger engine, the FX4S, was introduced. It was the first cab to carry LTI badges. The five-speed Rover manual gearbox was carried over with a revised, BW40 automatic transmission. Some draught proofing was added in the form of new mouldings to cover the door sills; the old toggle switches, no longer made, were replaced by rocker switches while the wipers and indicators were both operated from levers on the steering column.

The FX4S was distinguishable from the older models by its silver wheels and black rolled-steel bumpers. These were changed because the old tooling for the chrome bumpers had worn out and, as at the time the CR6 was in the offing, it was decided not to spend a lot of money on new tools for what was anticipated would be a short production run. Much was made in the brochure about the additional power of the 2.5-litre engine. It said: 'The climbing of hills in the FX4S with the new 2½-litre diesel engine and a full load is achieved with ease.' No petrol engine was offered. Again, the trim options were: FL (Fleetline), HL (Highline), and HLS (Highline Special).

A long wheelbase limousine

The brochure offered a limousine version, with 'a luxury interior to any standard of quality finish'. A long-wheelbase version was also available. No dimensions were given for the stretched version, but for practicality's sake it was most likely a four-door version, built by Tickford and by Robert Jankel, rather than a one-off six-door version by Woodall Nicholson.

ABOVE The arrival
of the Metrocab,
shown on the left
of this picture,
seriously worried
Carbodies. Here was
a very modern vehicle,
comfortable to drive,
with seating capacity
for five passengers,
and full wheelchair
accessibility.
(Barney Sharratt)

A new engine sought

The great advantage of the old Austin version was that its engine and manual gearbox were designed as an integrated unit and the BW35 automatic was matched by Borg-Warner themselves. One of the reasons for Carbodies' problems with the FX4R was that they had to mate the gearboxes to the engine and were given bad advice. It was vital that a new engine had compatible gearboxes, both manual and automatic, because London buyers were now choosing automatic transmission almost exclusively, while provincial buyers wanted manual gearboxes.

Carbodies asked engine specialists Ricardo Engineering to find them a new engine. They found one at Nissan in Japan, but the bad news was that it would soon go out of production. They would have a new engine ready, but not for some time. Would Carbodies wait? If the engine was good enough, and if a fully integrated automatic transmission was available for it, they said yes, they would, but LTI had a new problem to face, in the shape of a rival make, the MCW Metrocab.

The Metrocab

Since 1972, when the last Winchester taxicab was sold, the FX4 had had the market to itself. MCW had made a prototype Metrocab in the late 1960s, and it had run on test for two years with the fleet of the London General Cab Company, who were lined up to invest in it if they wanted it. But 'The General' said no, there were too many unanswered questions, too much development work to be dealt with before the cab would be up to scratch, and too many changes to be made in repair and servicing facilities, so the project was scrapped. Nevertheless, MCW returned to the idea of building a cab in the mid-1980s and an all-new Metrocab, with a modern glassfibre body seating five passengers (the FX4 had only ever been licensed to carry four in London) and, crucially, to meet forthcoming legislation, built-in wheelchair accessibility, was released in the spring of 1987. At last, the London cab trade had a choice of vehicles once more.

LEFT The London
Sterling had a number
of detail differences
from the FX4S, upon
which it was based.
Most were to comply
with US Federal safety
laws, such as additional
lights and impact-
absorbing bumpers.
(Murray Jackson)

The London Sterling and the London Coach

While the London taxi had been an international icon, it was a vehicle that the cab trades in other countries did not want. It was fine for London, but other towns and cities – New York, Berlin, Paris, Tokyo, Hong Kong, etc. – were content to run saloon cars. London had the PCO, which demanded a specific type of vehicle, and Mann & Overton, who supplied it, had a captive market. Nowhere else in the world had such a strict regime or such a thorough legislator. At Carbodies, the need to increase sales outside the Capital was vital, and in the early 1980s, an opportunity to secure a foothold in the biggest market of all, the USA arose. Specialist vehicle

LEFT To compete
with the Metrocab's
wheelchair accessibility
facility, LTI subsidiary
Carbodies Sales &
Service Ltd developed
this conversion for
the FX4R. The original
version had the door
hinged on the B-post,
but this later version
retained the original
door, although modified
to open a full 180°. The
partition could slide
forward to make room
for the wheelchair. This
rattled excessively and
the idea of a sliding
partition was abandoned.
(Taxi Newspaper Archive)

We proudly present the
new FX4 S-PLUS, a fully
developed state of the art, all
steel, tried, tested and proven
taxi now with many detailed
mechanical improvements
plus a completely new luxury
interior now licensed for five
passengers and a completely
new driver's cab and dash
board... putting the driver first!
And, of course, retaining that
most important of all
considerations, the high
visibility of the traditional
shape so loved by the
travelling public and the
millions of tourists to Britain.

HIGH PROFILE CLASSIC TAXI STYLING

maker Don Landers planned to build a version
of the FX4 from shipped-out parts, producing a
taxi version, the London Coach and a limousine
version, the luxurious London Sterling, which
would be a more compact vehicle than the USA's
monstrous stretch limos. It would have a 2.3-litre
Ford Pinto petrol engine and automatic gearbox.
Although it sold in modest numbers, the project
was undermined by a detrimental exchange rate
and poor reliability in comparison with the much-
preferred sedans and the ageing Checker cab.

The FX4S-Plus

The Metrocab had LTI seriously worried. All they
had to offer was the FX4S. This gave better
performance than the FX4R, albeit with an
increased noise level, but it had some draught
proofing. However, it was only an updated
version of a 30-year-old vehicle and had reliability
problems of its own, although this time not of
Carbodies' making, but Land Rover's. The FX4S
was introduced in 1985 and, with its improved
performance, sold better than the FX4R. Now,
to improve their sales and to try to compete on
better terms with the Metrocab, LTI revamped
the FX4S. They brought in a young designer,
Jevon Thorpe, who designed a stylish grey
interior which seated five passengers, together
with a completely new moulded grey dashboard
with modern instruments and switches.

The mechanical changes made for the new
model, named the FX4S-Plus, were overseen
by a new engineering director, Ed Osmond, who
had joined LTI from Reliant. They were confined
to telescopic shock absorbers and the new
GKN glassfibre Literide springs on the rear. New
colours were offered, but the trim options were
reduced to two: the basic FL (Fleetline) and the
HLS (Highline Special). The Plus was launched in

ABOVE The passenger compartment of the FX4S-Plus transformed the experience of riding in a London taxi. Velour seats were optional. *(London Taxi Company/London Vintage Taxi Association Archive)*

LEFT Along with the new grey interior, the new dashboard of the FX4S-Plus was a revelation to the cab trade. It showed that the management of the company was finally listening to the driver and not just the proprietor. *(Murray Jackson)*

LEFT LTI introduced the Fairway in February 1989, to great acclaim. This model, a 'Silver', has a vinyl roof, sliding sunroof and extra cost option wheel trims. Midnight blue had been a popular colour since its introduction in 1980. *(Author)*

September 1987 and was extremely well received by the trade, and sold well considering that it had to share the market with the Metrocab, but there was still no wheelchair accessibility. That would have to wait until the last minute, 1 February 1989, when a month after new legislation came in demanding all purpose-built cabs had this facility.

The Fairway

When wheelchair accessibility was finally available, it was part of the best version of the FX4 ever made, the Fairway. The chosen engine was a 2.7-litre Nissan diesel, minus the turbocharger as fitted when installed in Nissan's own light trucks and 4x4s. This would, in the fullness of time, help this simple but very well-engineered four-cylinder pushrod engine post mileages of over half a million. Obviously, in January 1989 when the Fairway was released, the trade could have no way of knowing this, but what everyone who test-drove it immediately discovered, was the power and the smoothness of the engine. They were delighted, and even for a time swallowed their complaints that it was still an FX4, an aged vehicle with all its potential for draughts, rattles, squeaks and water leaks. The engine came with the option of a four-speed

LEFT In a Fairway, more legroom was given to a passenger in a wheelchair by creating this dog-leg in the partition. The passenger sat facing rearwards, which was what the Transport Research Laboratory advised was the safest method. Just visible adjacent to the door pillar is the switch that operated the electric securing strap, itself visible below the tip-up seat. Passenger heater controls were located on the centre of the partition, between the back rests. *(Author)*

RIGHT The Nissan engine was even more of a surprise to the trade than the interior redesign. *(London Taxi Compan)*

automatic gearbox or a five-speed manual, both of an integrated design. Otherwise, the mechanical specification was the same as the S-Plus, with the same old BMC independent front suspension with lever arm shock absorbers, kingpins and swivel bushes and, sadly, the same drum brakes, but carrying over the telescopic shock absorbers and Literide springs on the rear.

Wheelchair accessibility was, of necessity, a compromise, the cab being an adaptation of an elderly design rather than a new model. The Transport Research Laboratory had deemed the safest way for a passenger in a wheelchair to travel in a cab was to face rearwards, which meant a dog-leg had to be incorporated into the partition, taking space from the luggage compartment. The rear floor had a peak in the middle which, along with the intrusion of the wheel arches, made manoeuvring the wheelchair into place difficult. To make it easier, LTI's engineers hinged the rear seat cushion so that it lifted up out of the way, and mounted both passenger doors on swan-neck hinges, so that the door opening was fully exposed and not partly covered as it was in previous models. Extending ramps to enable a wheelchair to be rolled into the cab were supplied, carried on the boot floor.

The interior was also an adaptation of that fitted to the S-Plus. Three new trim options were offered: Bronze, Silver and Gold and new colours, Sherwood Green and Champagne Beige were added to the S-Plus's options. Prices started at £14,273.80 for the Bronze manual, to £16,749.75 for the Gold with automatic transmission.

The Fairway Driver and Fairway 95

Over the next two years, sales of the Fairway exceeded all previous records for an FX4. There was a higher volume of provincial and even overseas sales too, and in 1990 annual production exceeded 3,000 for the first time in the vehicle's history. But the Fairway was a stopgap. Even before it was introduced, LTI's engineers, headed by managing director Barry Widdowson and engineering director Ed Osmond, were working on a completely new model. They knew that developing a new cab was going to be an expensive job, and they had to do it in what Osmond described as "bite-size chunks", developing the drivetrain and fitting it to the Fairway first.

The Nissan engine and gearbox had been the 'first bite', and the next task was to replace the Fairway's now ancient front suspension and brakes with a new, modern design. LTI engaged GKN to design a new front suspension system,

RIGHT The domed wheel trims of the Fairway Driver set it apart from the previous models. All-over advertising, known as a livery, became popular with owner-drivers and fleet proprietors alike, netting a decent sum of money up-front. When selling a new cab, Mann & Overton would offset the cost of the livery against the deposit. *(Barney Sharratt)*

using conventional wishbones and ball joints, but designed in such a way that disc brakes that AP Lockheed were developing in cooperation, could be fitted and still allow the mandatory tight turning circle. These, along with a new GKN back axle and wider rear brakes were installed on a new model, the Fairway Driver, which was introduced in February 1992. It was unfortunate for LTI that this coincided with a collapse in the British economy, for although the Fairway Driver was well received – even better than the original Fairway – sales were down by about 40 per cent on those of 1990.

In 1993, the Driver Plus, a revised model, was introduced, with a split rear seat, where each half could be raised to enable a wheelchair to be turned round, but one-half left up to accommodate the wheelchair-bound passenger's feet, but allowed a passenger to sit facing forward. There was a new design of partition, with a lift-up flap for the passenger to pay the driver. This was done because outside London,

ABOVE LTI's promotional photograph of the Fairway 95. Note the wheelchair symbols on the 'Taxi' sign. *(London Taxi Company/*Taxi *Newspaper Archive)*

LEFT The Fairway Driver brake and front suspension system, designed by GKN and AP Lockheed. *(*Taxi *Newspaper Archive)*

ABOVE The Fairway 95. The vinyl roof and sunshine roof were no longer offered as part of a trim package, although they were available as optional extras. Black was still the most popular colour for London cabs. *(Author)*

RIGHT The Fairway 95 featured a split rear seat, to enable wheelchairs with more prominent stirrups to be accommodated, and still allow a passenger to sit on the rear seat. The red grab handles and edgings on the seat cushion are to aid the partially sighted. *(Author)*

passengers expected to pay before getting out, whereas in the capital, it was customary to pay the driver after getting out. Now, a lot of London passengers had begun to pay the driver before getting out. However, the flap caused a draught around the driver's neck and was universally disliked. When the next version, the Fairway 95, came out in the summer of 1995, LTI changed the partition opening to one on the nearside glass and would retrofit this on request to the Driver Plus.

Provincial sales

The Fairway was by far the most successful FX4 to be sold outside London. LTI had campaigned to sell London-type cabs to provincial markets, using wheelchair accessibility as the main selling point, to persuade many licensing authorities to adopt it. This was opposed by many in the provincial taxi trade, who objected to having these vehicles, which they insisted were too expensive to buy and maintain, unsuitable for their area, and unnecessary, as the wheelchair-bound population in their area was too small to justify the purchase of special vehicles. Nevertheless, against this opposition, many provincial licensing authorities

adopted London-type cabs. It achieved what LTI had wanted and, with the adoption of spares distribution through Unipart, established a foothold for their cabs in previously untapped provincial markets. It also paved the way for Metrocab and, in time, a range of van conversion taxis with full wheelchair facility, which provided not only direct competition, but threatened the existence of the one thing that had deterred other makers from challenging Mann & Overton's prominence in London, the 25ft turning circle.

The end

At long last, the FX4 finally came to the end of its production life in 1997. The long-term development of a new model, which had begun a decade before, had come to fruition and the last Fairway 95 rolled off the tracks at the Coventry factory in 1997. The replacement model would be the TX1, which had an all-new body, built on a chassis developed from the Fairway. Its styling, however, was copied deliberately from the FX4, to please the many new overseas customers and to preserve that timeless shape designed more than forty years before by Eric Bailey.

ABOVE The last Fairway and the first TX1. It was always said, years ago, that if you lasted a fortnight at Carbodies, you were there for life. This picture proves it, as the five men seen here, from left: Dave Burnham, Bob Barker, Barry Cardin, Peter Lee and Ron Wilkins, worked on the very first FX4s and the very last Fairways. Between them, they clocked up an astonishing 209 years' service! *(London Taxi Company/Taxi Newspaper Archive)*

RIGHT A surprising success story was the sales of Fairways to the home of Mercedes-Benz, Germany. The partition added extra safety to German taxi drivers, who were being subjected to a growing number of attacks and even murders. Maintenance was carried out by specialist taxi service centres. *(Stanley Roth Collection)*

RIGHT Portugal was another country that bought Fairways. This two-tone Fairway Driver went to Lisbon. *(Stanley Roth Collection)*

LEFT This special cab was commissioned by HRH the Prince of Wales to commemorate the Silver Jubilee of HM Queen Elizabeth II in 1977. *(London Vintage Taxi Association Archive)*

Export models

Different versions of the Fairway were sold worldwide too, to countries as far afield as Singapore, Portugal, Spain, Germany, Kenya and Taiwan. Some were taxi versions, while others were limousines. Several were sold to Japan as mobile offices. Japan's traffic was so bad that travelling took such a long time and executives found it better to conduct their business while trying to travel!

Special versions of the FX4 and FL2

Commercial applications

The FX3 chassis had been made available in 'driveaway' form, with the bare chassis plus bonnet, front wings and windscreen, to outside coachbuilders. The most prominent versions had been the vans used by London's three evening newspapers, and there were several

LEFT The 'Driveaway' chassis provided a base for outside coachbuilders to build different bodies. *(NMM)*

RIGHT After the success of the FX3 newspaper vans, it was hoped that the FX4 would be a good replacement. It was a failure. Its unreliability was not helped by the growth of economical steel-bodied vans from the major manufacturers. *(Chris Hodge Trucks)*

BELOW Just like the newspaper vans, this single Royal Mail van failed to live up to expectations. *(British Postal Museum & Archive)*

hearses and wood-bodied shooting brakes made. Austin decided that a driveaway version of the FX4 would be offered too. The London *Evening News* commissioned some vans to be built on this chassis, but unlike the FX3 vans, which were powered by petrol engines with manual gearboxes, the diesel automatic FX4 vans were slow as well as expensive, and the automatic transmission proved as troublesome in use as it had been in the taxi.

The Royal Mail experimented with one van version of the FX4. Fitted with a box body, it was put on trial in south east London in February 1967, but it appears to have been unstable when fully loaded. It was moved to Coventry, where it carried lighter loads until it was decommissioned in the mid-1970s.

The London clothing industry, the 'rag trade', at one time being based to the north of Oxford Street, bought a few gown vans based on FX4 chassis, trusting that the turning circle would ease the progress of deliveries through the Capital's hopelessly congested streets. These only amounted to a few vehicles as they were more expensive than those built on other bases, and offered no financial advantage.

The FL1 chassis had provided a base for an economical hearse, and likewise the FX4 did too, with bodies supplied by Thomas Startin and Alpe & Saunders. The petrol engine was by far the more popular choice for both the hearse and accompanying FL2 Hire Cars.

Exclusive and exotic cabs and Hire Cars

Stretch limousines

At least four stretch limousines have been built on FX4 chassis: three with four doors and one with no fewer than six. Two of the four-door cars were by Tickford, one in gunmetal and the other in maroon. The bodies were extended by fitting an extra panel between the front and rear doors. The rearward-facing seats were fixed down and the space between them filled with a walnut-veneered cocktail cabinet, a sound system, television and a video player. The gunmetal version was ordered by American Dr Bill Wallace, who fitted a Ford Pinto engine, of a similar type used in the American-built London Coach and London Sterling.

ABOVE The FX4/FL2 was not as popular a choice as the base for a hearse as the FX3/FL1 chassis had been. With the arrival of cheaper, large unit-construction cars the FX4 was outpriced and outclassed. This example by Thomas Startin Jnr was rare. *(Classic Hearse Register)*

BELOW This gunmetal stretch limo was built by Tickford and sold to an American client. *(Bill Powell)*

Another four-door version was built to a similar configuration to the Tickford cars, by Robert Jankel, the people behind the Panther sports car. All of these were built on the FX4R chassis. The biggest version was the six-door, built by hearse builder Woodall Nicholson of Yorkshire. This has three doors each side and three rows of forward-facing bench seats, upholstered in velour. Based on an FX4S chassis, it was built to ferry passengers between Birmingham New Street station and the National Exhibition Centre, when the Motor Show was held there in 1985.

ABOVE The Tickford stretch limo included the almost mandatory cocktail cabinet and stereo sound system, plus leather interior.
(Bill Powell)

RIGHT The Tickford limousines proved hard to sell. This one featured a similar interior to the gunmetal example.
(Steve Tillyer)

RIGHT A similar body to that produced by Tickford was this by Robert Jankel Associates, the company that built the Panther sports car.
(Robert Jankel)

ABOVE This six-door stretch was built by hearse builders Woodall Nicholson for LTI to use at the Birmingham Motor Show to ferry passengers to and from the venue. *(London Taxi Company/Taxi Newspaper Archive)*

RIGHT The interior of the six-door stretch was trimmed in velour. *(London Taxi Company/Taxi Newspaper Archive)*

A special FL2 for BSA

Carbodies was owned by BSA for almost two decades. Another of its constituent companies was Daimler, but when this prestigious company was sold to Jaguar in 1960, BSA found itself without an in-house limousine builder who could build cars for their management's use and for

ABOVE The special FL2 built for BSA by Carbodies. The three men shown are Mr H.R. Niven, BSA's company secretary, Bill Lucas, Carbodies Ltd's director and general manager, and Jake Donaldson, Carbodies' engineering director. *(London Taxi Company)*

RIGHT The letters of the number plate stand for 'William Thomas Lucas', Bill Lucas of Carbodies Ltd, who had this special cab built. *(Steve Tillyer)*

other tasks. Thus they commissioned a special FL2 Hire Car that would serve to transfer visitors to BSA's headquarters from Birmingham New Street station.

The *Steering Wheel* FX4

The man responsible for overseeing the production of this FL2 was Bill Lucas. After BSA had sold out to Manganese Bronze Holdings, Lucas built himself a special cab. It was a petrol automatic based on an early 1970s chassis. Fully kitted out with every luxury item available, it served as a mobile advert for the company's products. Lucas later sold the cab in the 1970s to Lenham Publicity Ltd, owners of *The Steering Wheel* taxi trade journal, who used it for promotional purposes of their own.

Nubar Gulbenkian

Without doubt the most exotic versions of the FX4 were the two limousines built in the 1960s by FLM Panelcraft for Armenian oil magnate Nubar Gulbenkian. As well as buying some extravagantly styled Rolls-Royces, he had already run a customised FX3, the sides of which were decorated with basketwork, similar to that fitted to a Delaunay-Belleville limousine owned by his mother before the Great War. His first FX4 was similarly styled, but the second had Regency stripes and stylised front wings and bonnet. Gulbenkian was fond of displaying his wealth, as his cars demonstrated. He was, it was said, as profligate with his money as his father had been parsimonious. When asked why he chose to ride in a custom taxi rather than one of his Rolls-Royces, he famously replied: "I'm told it can turn on a sixpence, whatever that may be!"

Rex Hunt and the Falkland Islands

One FX4 that was unknown to the public until 1983, was used as official transport for the then Governor of the Falkland Islands, Rex Hunt. When the Islands were invaded by the

LEFT The interior of 'WTL 9'. A cocktail cabinet sits where the tip-up seats would be in a normal FX4. Certainly the girls from the office of Lenham Publicity, the owners of *The Steering Wheel* who acquired the cab, seem to enjoy being cosseted in the plush interior. *(Steve Tillyer)*

ABOVE The second of Nubar Gulbenkian's flamboyant FX4 limousines. This had Regency stripes on the rear of the body, whereas his first FX4 was decorated with basketwork. (*London Vintage Taxi Association Archive*)

ABOVE The former Governor of the Falkland Islands, Rex (now Sir Rex) Hunt with the FX4 that became a symbol of British defiance following the Argentinean invasion in 1982. (*Imperial War Museum*)

Argentinian forces, the venerable taxi became a symbol of Britishness and British defiance. It was retired some time after, but brought out of retirement in October 2004 to serve as a wedding car when the Governor, Mr Howard Pearce CVO married his Dutch fiancée, Caroline Thomée.

The Crown Prince of Tonga

The Crown Prince of Tonga, HRH Prince Putouto'a, was a great fan of the FX4. In 1996, he took delivery of a specially trimmed version with a 2.4-litre Nissan petrol engine, deep carpets, cocktail cabinet, CD player and wood cappings to the doors. Large in stature, the prince enjoyed the easy access the cab gave him, especially as it was the only production vehicle he could get into while wearing his ceremonial sword.

Other famous owners

The late Sir Laurence Olivier bought two FL2 Hire Cars in succession. He was, he told Carbodies when he ordered them, always performing one play, rehearsing a second and learning the script for a third, and a chauffeur-driven FL2 provided a private mobile office in which he could study his scripts. He had the cabs trimmed in burgundy Bedford cord.

Comedian and actor Sydney James, star of the film *Carry on Cabby* and his own TV series, *Taxi* bought one for his own use, while other, more recent well-known FX4 owners include HRH The Duke of Edinburgh and actor Stephen Fry.

ABOVE A team from LTI polish the last FX4 model to be shipped to the Crown Prince of Tonga. Although it is based on a Fairway Driver, it had a straight partition, rather than the cab's dog-leg. (*London Taxi Company/* Taxi *Newspaper Archive*)

LEFT The interior of the FX4 built for the Crown Prince of Tonga. Opulent, as befits its owner's status. (*London Taxi Company/*Taxi *Newspaper Archive*)

Chapter Two

Anatomy of the FX4

The Austin FX4 was the first truly modern London taxi of its time, in its overall design and mechanical make-up, but compared with contemporary motor vehicles, there was nothing about it that was revolutionary, or even innovative. The secret of its longevity was that it was a robust, mechanically well-engineered, entirely serviceable vehicle, designed to do a particular job, using as many available parts as possible.

LEFT Mounting the body of a Fairway Driver on to its chassis at the LTI Carbodies factory in Coventry. *(London Taxi Company/Taxi Newspaper Archive)*

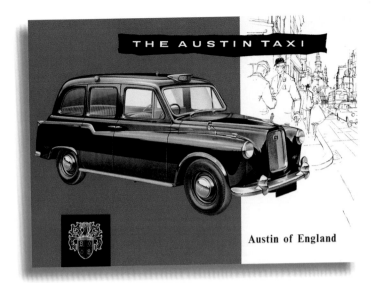

THE AUSTIN TAXI

Austin of England

ABOVE The first
Austin FX4 brochure
illustrated the general
layout of the cab and
its modern shape, as
well as all its original
details: the roof-
mounted indicators,
straight door handles,
and shield-type
grille badge.
(Author's Collection)

BELOW Although
it looks like a taxi
without the roof light,
there were important
differences between
the FL2 Hire Car and
the FX4 taxi.
(Author's Collection)

The FX4 was designed for a particular purpose, and to meet specific design criteria, the Metropolitan Police Conditions of Fitness, which required all cabs (the word 'taxi' was not used officially by the licensing authority, the PCO, until 2000), to have a limousine configuration with a partition dividing the driver from the passengers. The FX4 was the first full-production London-type model to have four full doors, the first to have both a diesel engine and an automatic transmission fitted as standard from its introduction, and the first to have independent front suspension. All these features, with the exception of the automatic gearbox, were found on the revolutionary Birch prototype of 1956, but that cab did not go into production.

The FX4 was also the first to have a body made entirely of pressed steel. The preceding Austin model, the FX3, had a certain amount of wood in its frame, the Beardmore MkVII had a coachbuilt body with aluminium panels over

an ash frame, and the Oxford of 1947 had a composite body with pressed steel panels over ash, similar to the pre-war Morris-Commercial cabs.

Model types

Because the FX4 was in production for so long, there were many changes in its specification brought about by what engines and other components were available. This resulted in several different models being produced. The taxis can be divided broadly into five separate groups. There are also five different Hire Car versions, with optional petrol and diesel engines fitted at various times.

The taxi models were:
- The original Austin FX4, built from 1958 to 1969.
- The face-lifted Austin FX4, nicknamed the 'new shape' by the trade, which can be subdivided into the 2.2-litre diesel (late 1969 to late 1971), the first 2.5-litre diesel model (late 1971 to May 1974), and the revised version of the 2.5 diesel, adapted to meet European safety rules (May 1974 to September 1982, including the identical Carbodies FX4D).
- Carbodies models with Rover engines, including the FX4R, FX4S and FX4S-Plus.
- Carbodies Fairway and Fairway Driver models.
- The London Coach, built for the USA between 1985 and 1987.

The Hire Car and limousine models were:
- The original Austin FL2D diesel, built from 1958 to 1969, and the FL2 (petrol) built from 1962 to 1969.
- The face-lifted Austin FL2D diesel, built from 1969 to 1976, and FL2 petrol, built from 1969 to 1972.
- The Carbodies FL2 London Limousine.
- The Carbodies Fairway and Fairway Driver, offered as special limousine versions.
- The London Sterling limousine, built for the USA between 1985 and 1987.
- The FL2 Hire Car, London Limousine and commercial variants.

AUSTIN

DIESEL HIRE CAR

ABOVE An original-type Austin FX4, probably the first bought by the London General Cab Company. *(Andrew Hall)*

LEFT The small stop/tail lights were also used on the Jaguar XK120 and XK140. *(Author)*

BELOW LEFT The revised Austin brochure illustration of 1969, with wing-mounted indicators. *(London Vintage Taxi Association Archive)*

BELOW RIGHT The FL2 received the same changes in 1969 as did the taxi. This brochure is from 1972, offering the new 2.5-litre diesel and the 2.2-litre petrol engine. *(London Vintage Taxi Association Archive)*

Austin Taxi and Hire Car

Body

The construction had stayed the same throughout the production life, this being all-steel with four doors and six lights. (In USA parlance, a seven-window body.) The main part of the body, consisting of roof, cant rails, scuttle, sills, boot and the structural members, was assembled as a unit rear of the front wings, with inner and outer sills, and outer rear wings. The doors and boot lid were bolted on to the body before it was mounted on the chassis. The front wing assemblies and bonnet were bolted on after the body was mounted.

The doors were built from an inner structural shell, with an outer skin crimped over the edges of the shell. The front doors were hinged on the A-posts, while the rear, passenger, doors were bolted to the C-posts. Until 1989, and the introduction of the Fairway, the doors on all models were prevented from opening too wide by an internally fitted check strap, originally leather, but later changed to webbing. Fairway doors were prevented from opening too wide by a metal strap extending from within the door.

All the main windows in the doors open, sliding vertically. The original mechanism was a constant-balance spring, dampened by felt-lined rubber channels. An accessory electric window conversion was offered for the platform door and was fitted on a small number of models built between 1979 and 1987. These were identified by the bulge on the door that houses the motor. From 1987, electric front windows were offered on higher-specification models of the FX4S-Plus and the motor was completely concealed within the door. Front electric windows became a standard fitting from 1995, with electrically operated rear windows offered as a dealer-fitted option. Models built between spring 1974 and the end of 1988 had opening quarterlights in the front doors.

All glass, except the rear window, was flat, and was held in place by rubber mouldings. The windscreen of the Fairway had a slightly larger glass area than earlier models, although the aperture was the same. This was achieved by sitting the glass on top of the rubber moulding, instead of sitting it within, as was done on previous models.

The passenger compartment was divided from the driver's area by a partition, located in line with the B-posts. The partition was

ABOVE LTI took the Fairway all the way to the Royal and Ancient Golf Club at St Andrews, Scotland, for its launch. The connection between the club and the cab's name was completely lost on the trade as a whole. *(London Taxi Company/Taxi Newspaper Archive)*

LEFT The London Coach was supplied without the standard roof sign, which allowed US operators to fit their own type of sign. *(Don Smith)*

BELOW The Fairway Driver is easily identified by its domed wheel trims and expanded mesh grille. *(Barney Sharratt)*

Carbodies Fairway Driver

1. Rear brake drum
2. Rear leaf spring
3. Differential
4. Body outrigger
5. Chassis side member
6. Jacking point
7. Exhaust pipe
8. Propeller shaft
9. Brake disc
10. Brake hose
11. Upper suspension wishbone
12. Telescopic shock absorber and coil spring
13. Steering arm
14. Steering lever
15. Lower suspension wishbone
16. Power steering box
17. Steering column crash link
18. Power steering fluid reservoir
19. Fuel filter
20. Master cylinder
21. Brake fluid reservoir
22. Brake servo
23. Heater
24. Windscreen wiper motor
25. Battery
26. Air cleaner
27. Venturi hose
28. Engine oil filler cap
29. Radiator
30. Viscous fan
31. Horn
32. Number plate mount
33. Energy-absorbing bumper
34. Front bumper end cap
35. Fuel cut-off switch
36. Nearside steering idler
37. Front indicator
38. Headlamp with integral sidelight
39. Radiator expansion tank
40. Glass partition
41. 'For Hire' sign
42. Fuel tank

TAXI

constructed of square tube and contributed to the structural strength of the body. A luggage platform was provided by the driver's side, separated from the driver's seat by a low partition and accessed by the external door. Plywood panels inset into the floor of the passenger compartment allowed for inspection of the upper surfaces of the chassis.

The bonnet was made of a single pressing, with a vee-shape cut out, bent at a right angle and welded back together. Each front wing was composed of two pieces, an inner and an outer, which were bolted together. Inner wings completed the structural assembly and were braced by a frame at the forward end that also held the radiator. A flat valance was bolted to the front of the chassis members, between the front edge of the wings and the bumper. The boot lid comprised an inner shell and outer skin, hinged at the lower edge and prevented from opening beyond 45° by two plastic-covered wire ropes. The boot lid of the FL2 could open to a horizontal position, and was held thus by two folding flat steel straps. The number plate was housed on the boot lid. On the taxi, the licence plate issued by the various licensing authorities that accepted the FX4, were screwed to the boot lid below the number plate.

Exterior fittings

With a vehicle that had been in production for so long, with few changes apparent to the casual observer, it was the details that identified each variant. Each of the five taxi and five Hire Car variants can be identified as follows.

BELOW The windscreen fitted to all models prior to 1989, which was inset into the moulding. *(Author)*

BELOW RIGHT The Fairway windscreen, which sat on top of the moulding, allowing a larger glass area. *(London Taxi Company/ Taxi Newspaper Archive)*

The original diesel FX4D and FL2D (1958 to 1969), and petrol Austin FX4 and FL2 (1962 to 1969)

These models were at first distinguished by roof-mounted limpet-type flashing indicator lights (omitted from the FL2 from 1962), combined stop/tail lights with red lens and integral reflector, chromium-plated sidelights mounted on top of the front wings, short, straight exterior door handles, full-width cast aluminium window pulls, and darkened 'purdah' glass in the rear window. (The FL2 rear window was clear safety glass.) On the boot lid, the number plate light was originally mounted below the plate and the 'Austin' name appeared in script on the offside. A vertical chromium-plated crest was fitted to the bonnet, containing the Austin coat of arms in a plastic badge. The mesh grille had a thick chrome surround and a centrally mounted, trapezoid Austin badge. The door handles were of a straight, pull-down type. The trim around the window glass was finished in black paint.

The bumpers and overriders were chromium plated. The sills were trimmed with an alloy casting with a black rubber insert. The bonnet catch, visible on the front valance was a slide-across type with a chromium-plated handle, with the safety catch concealed under the front of the bonnet. (Until 1990, all bonnet catches were external, to comply with PCO requirements to allow its inspectors to examine a vehicle without the owner or driver being present.) A single chrome Lucas fog lamp was fitted as standard on the valance, and the roof sign had the legend 'For hire' cut out of a steel

stencil, set in front of an amber glass lens. No roof sign was fitted to Hire Cars.

From April 1960, a simpler type of grille with no separate chrome surround was fitted and the large Austin badge was replaced by a simple one with 'Austin' in script, fixed to the nearside of the grille. In September 1960 new, stronger cranked exterior door handles were fitted, as the original ones were too fragile. In late 1967, the original chrome sidelights were discarded and sealed-beam headlight units with integral sidelights, as used on the BMC Mini, were fitted.

A small number of accessories were offered, including 'rimbellisher' wheel trims, an additional fog light, and a rubbing strip along the front wings and front doors. Two additional body colours were offered in the catalogue, carmine red, and white. Other colours were available to special order, but very few customers chose any other colour besides black.

The face-lifted Austin FX4 and FX4D (late 1969 to Spring 1982), and Carbodies FX4D (Spring to September 1982)

For 1969, the FX4 underwent a major rework, to address some of the problems found with the original model. Tail lights from the BMC 1100/1300 MkII range replaced the small triangular stop/tail lights, and the roof-mounted limpet indicators, with the inner and outer rear wings, were remodelled to accommodate them. Small circular orange front indicators of the type used on the FL2 from around 1964, were fitted below the

headlights on the front face of the inner wings. Small rectangular repeater indicators were fitted to the front wings. The lens of the roof sign was changed to amber plastic with the word 'TAXI' painted on it.

A new circular, flush-mounted bonnet badge was fitted, with a chrome surround and bearing the Austin coat of arms set in clear plastic. Clear glass replaced the dark 'purdah' glass and the trim around the window glass was given a bright metal finish. Thick, ribbed rubber mouldings replaced the original alloy sill coverings, which in turn were replaced in 1970 by a ribbed bright alloy pressing. A small rectangular 'British Leyland' symbol, silver on blue, was fixed to each front wing. In 1973, a small selection of new colours, in addition to the original extra-cost choices of carmine red and white, were offered, including Aconite (a bright mauve colour) and dark blue.

From May 1974, in line with the demands of European legislation, push-button door handles replaced the cranked type, no badge was fitted to the bonnet, and opening quarter-lights were used. In early 1977, composite rubber

RIGHT A much stronger cranked-type external door handle was fitted from 1960. The hard rubber blocks, to stop passengers' clothing being caught on the handle, was introduced in 1970. *(Author)*

RIGHT The original chromium-plated interior door handles were quite substantial. The ash trays less so, and were often inclined to stick, making the emptying of them difficult. This may seem a trivial matter, but when fleet cab washers and cleaners had dozens to do every day, every little helps, as the saying goes. *(Author)*

overriders replaced chromium-plated steel ones, along with an optional heated rear window. Later that year, the heated rear window became a standard fitting and a chromium driver's door mirror and nearside rectangular wing mirror replaced the twin circular type. Twin rectangular Transit wing mirrors were an optional extra. In January 1978, a rectangular chromium-plated badge bearing the Austin name in black capital letters replaced the Austin script badge on the grille and boot lid. New colours offered included bright blue, brown and grass green. The Leyland badge was not fitted from 1979.

RIGHT 'Rimbellisher' wheel trims were bought mainly by owner-drivers and although not cheap, added a touch of style to the cab. The Austin script initial 'A' is just visible on the centre of the hub cap. *(Author)*

FAR RIGHT A cheaper option was the 'turbo'-style wheel trims, which were on the fragile side and tended to rattle as they aged. *(Author)*

In late 1980, a wide range of accessories were offered. These included a vinyl roof, a hinged tinted glass sunroof, which had only just been approved by the PCO, optional rear fog lights hung below the bumper, and manually operated reversing lights, fitted to the rear quarter panels, and a new colour, Midnight Blue.

In 1980, Carbodies acquired the intellectual rights to the FX4 and began manufacture in their own name. The Austin badges were replaced by a single square black plastic 'Carbodies' item on the nearside of the boot lid, a rectangular black plastic 'Carbodies' badge and the new company logo were fixed to the grille, and the Austin 'A' script was no longer stamped on the hubcaps. The Carbodies FX4 was identical in every other respect to the last Austin model. Throughout the 1970s, the FL2 Hire Car was upgraded in the same way as the FX4.

The FX4R, FL2 London Limousine and FX4Q

Visual differences between a Carbodies FX4D, FX4R and FX4Q were very minor. The FX4R was identified by a pair of black plastic badges with silver lettering fitted on the boot lid, and a single badge fitted to the grille. The nearside boot and grille badges were of the same, long rectangular style, while the offside badge read 'FX4R'. Keener eyes can spot a lower ride height at the front, created by lowering blocks placed against the front axle beam.

The FX4Q was almost identical to the FX4R, except that it carried a single plastic FX4Q badge on the boot lid, with silver lettering on black. In 1983, corrosion-free front indicator lights with screw-on lenses replaced the older type, which had lenses located within a lip on the rubber gasket. To accommodate the slightly larger power

ABOVE The features of the so-called 'new shape' Austin continued, with minor detail changes, for almost 30 years. The new tail light clusters were, along with the clear back window, the main external changes. (*Author*)

steering box, the bonnet pressing was given two small vertical bulges at the lower end either side of the grille.

The trim options on the FX4R were offered as three separate packages: FL (Fleetline), HL (Highline), and HLS (Highline Special).

FL2R London Limousine

London Limousine models were distinguished by the absence of a taxi sign on the roof and different badges, but otherwise they had the same external fittings as the taxi.

FX4S and FX4S-Plus

The most noticeable differences between the FX4R and the FX4S were the latter's black rolled-steel bumpers with rubber end caps and inserts, and the silver wheels. Also, the windscreen wipers were finished in matt black instead of chromium plate. The badges carried the new 'London Taxis International' logo front and rear and the legend 'FX4S'. The FX4S-Plus was similar to the FX4S, but with an extra badge on the grille with the word 'Plus' and the casings of the door mirrors, one on each front door, were plastic. There were three trim options for the FX4S: Fleetline, HL and HLS, but just two for the FX4S-Plus: the FL and HLS.

Carbodies Fairway and Fairway Driver

The differences between the FX4S-Plus and the Fairway were in the grille, with a finer mesh and no badge, heavy black plastic door handles, fixed front quarterlights, plastic-cased door mirrors of a different design, and different badges on the boot lid. On the left of the boot lid was the word 'Fairway' in script and on the right, a plastic badge with the letters 'TD27' and either 'Bronze', 'Silver' or 'Gold' to denote the trim option. The Fairway Driver and Fairway 95 were more distinctive, with domed plastic wheel trims and an expanded mesh grille. Fairway Driver badges were similar to the original Fairway model, with the word 'Driver' below 'Fairway', while the Fairway 95 had just the Fairway script and the number '95'.

The London Coach and London Sterling

These were the most distinctive of all FX4 models, with additional lights mounted on the front and rear wings, and impact-absorbing bumpers to comply with US Federal legislation, plus heavy-duty plastic

RIGHT Push-button door handles appeared in 1974. Black rubber overriders and a new, rectangular 'Austin' name badge were fitted to the Austin FX4 from 1977 onwards.
(Author)

ABOVE This 1981 Austin has some of the add-ons that were proving popular from late 1980 onwards, including a vinyl roof, reversing lights, rear fog light, a rubbing strip on the front wings and doors, as well as the ever-popular Rimbellishers. One change, made to this cab and to a few others that were owner-driven, was to eventually replace the black rubber overriders with the older-type chrome ones. *(Author)*

LEFT The FX4Q differed little from the Austin FX4 or the Carbodies FX4R. Again, this example has had the rubber overriders replaced by early chrome ones. *(Author)*

door handles and an extruded mesh grille. The London Sterling, as a limousine model, had a vinyl roof with limousine-style privacy windows, pinstriping, stainless steel wheel covers, tinted glass, and a slatted grille insert.

Chassis frame

The chassis frame was made of pressed steel, of welded construction with U-section side members. The frame was braced by a substantial X-member and there were two full-width ladder-type cross members at the front, plus a third at the rear and two smaller cross-members adjacent to the clutch housing, located on the X-member. There were four body mounts, extending outwards from the main chassis side rails. Two jacking points, consisting of tubular brackets, extended outwards from each side, adjacent to the passenger doors.

Engine

All diesel engines fitted were four-cylinder, overhead-valve water-cooled types, made variously by Austin, Rover, Nissan and Kalaskai Diesel of India. Austin petrol engines were found on production FX4s and FL2s, and Rover ohv petrol engines may be found on FX4R and FL2R models. There was a single known example of a BL O-Series petrol engine fitted to an FX4R. The London Coach and London Sterling were fitted with the 2.3-litre Ford Pinto petrol engine.

Austin 2.2-litre diesel
(1958 to 1969)

This engine was found in the original model and in the 'new shape' models up to late 1971. It was derived from the Austin A70 petrol engine and was a four-cylinder, indirect injection in-line diesel with a capacity of 2,178cc (132.7cu in). The crankshaft had three main bearings. Two variations of this engine were fitted, the 22E with the

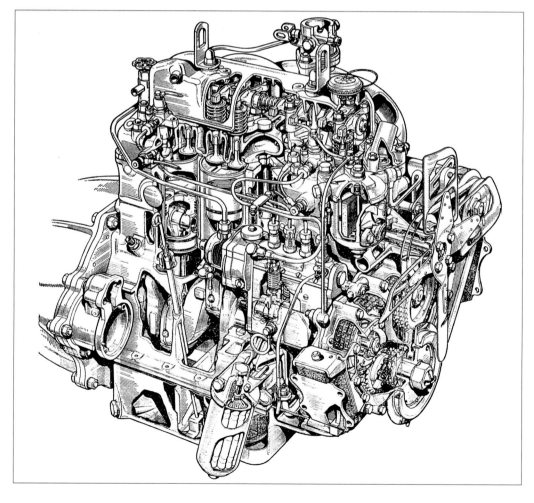

RIGHT A cutaway of the 2.2-litre Austin diesel engine in its original form, with the in-line injector pump. This was later replaced with a radial pump. Both 2.2-litre engines used cartridge-type oil filters as shown here, whereas the 2.5-litre used a canister type.
(Author's Collection)

automatic transmission and the 22K with manual transmission. Both produced 55bhp at 3,500rpm. The block and crankcase were of cast iron and were integral. Alloy pistons with combustion chambers in the crown were used, with three compression rings and one oil control ring.

The cast-iron cylinder head was detachable and held on by studs and nuts. It was of a Ricardo 'Comet' design, with a separate pre-combustion chamber. Exhaust and inlet ports were on the same side. There were two valves per cylinder, operated by a single camshaft on the nearside, running in three bearings and driven by a duplex chain. The tappets were cylinder-type and the rockers were forged, with clearance adjusted by a screw and locking nut. Covers for the rockers and tappet chest were cast alloy and the timing cover was of pressed steel. Lubrication was pressurised by an eccentric rotor, and the fuel filter was a full-flow type with a cartridge-type element.

Austin 2.2-litre petrol
(1962 to 1973)

This was a four-cylinder, in-line petrol engine with a capacity of 2,199cc (134.1cu in), producing 55.9bhp at 3,750rpm. Although this engine had a capacity close to its diesel derivative, the bore and stroke were different. The cast-iron block

and crankcase were integral and the crankshaft had three main bearings. There were two types fitted, the 22Z and 22ZA. Alloy pistons with three compression rings and one oil control ring were fitted. The detachable cast-iron cylinder head was held down by studs and nuts and had two valves per cylinder, operated by a single chain-drive camshaft on the nearside, running in three bearings.

Exhaust and inlet ports were both on the nearside. The tappets were cylinder-type and the rockers were forged, with clearance adjusted by a screw and locking nut. Covers for the rockers and tappet chest were cast alloy and the timing cover was of pressed steel. Lubrication was pressurised by an eccentric rotor-type pump driven by a skew gear off the camshaft, and the fuel filter was a full-flow type with a cartridge-type element. It had one single-choke Zenith 42 VIS or 30 VM6 carburettor, supplied by an AC Delco mechanical lift pump, driven off the camshaft, and a Lucas 25D/4 distributor, supplying a single spark plug per cylinder.

Austin 2.52-litre diesel
(late 1971 to Autumn 1982)

This engine, the 25V, had a capacity of 2,520cc and produced 63bhp at 3,500rpm. It was found in the 'new shape' model from late 1971 up to the

RIGHT The 2.5-litre
diesel engine came
with a pressurised
cooling system, an air
cleaner with a paper
filter, an alternator,
and a single battery.
(Author)

BELOW The offside
of the 2.3-litre Land
Rover diesel engine.
Note the location of
the injector pump,
mounted vertically.
(Author's Collection)

Spring of 1982, and in the short-lived Carbodies FX4D (Spring to Autumn 1982). It was produced for the new Austin-Morris EA350 and its design and construction were the same as the 2.2-litre engine. The rocker cover was made of pressed steel rather than alloy, and the oil filter was of a canister type.

Land Rover 2.3-litre diesel
(FX4R and FL2 London Limousine)
(October 1982 to Spring 1985)
This was a four-cylinder, indirect injection in-line diesel with a capacity of 2,286cc (139 cu in) and produced 62bhp at 4,000rpm.

The block and crankcase were of cast iron and were integral, and the crankshaft had five main bearings. Alloy pistons, each with three compression and one oil control ring, and combustion chambers in the crown were fitted. The cast-iron cylinder head was of a Ricardo 'Comet' design, held down by bolts. A glow plug pre-heated each pre-combustion chamber for easy starting. Exhaust and inlet ports were on the same side. There were two valves per cylinder, operated by a single camshaft on the nearside, running in four bearings and driven by a duplex chain with a spring-loaded tensioner. The tappets were cylinder-type and the rockers were forged, with clearance adjusted by a screw and locking nut. Covers for the rockers and tappet chest were cast alloy and the timing cover was of pressed steel. Lubrication was pressurised by a gear-type pump driven by a skew gear off the camshaft, and the full-flow oil filter was a canister type.

Land Rover petrol
(FX4R and FL2 London Limousine)
(October 1982 to Spring 1985)
This engine was offered at the same time as the 2.3-litre Land Rover diesel. Maximum power was 77bhp at 4,250rpm. Its construction was the same as the diesel engine, with the exception of the pistons, which were flat crown. Their cubic capacities were identical. It had a single-choke Zenith

361V carburettor fed by a mechanical lift pump driven off the camshaft, and a Lucas 45D distributor. Lubrication was the same type as the diesel.

One single FX4R was fitted with 2-litre BL O-Series ohc petrol engine, two were fitted with Land Rover diesel automatics with overdrive, and one Land Rover petrol automatic with overdrive was made.

Ford Pinto (London Coach and London Sterling)
(1985 to 1987)

This engine was one of a number of standard types fitted to US Ford cars during the 1970s and 1980s and was an in-line four-cylinder, water-cooled petrol engine of 2,302cc (140.477cu in) with a single overhead cam, driven by a toothed rubber belt and a five-bearing crank. It produced 88bhp at 4,800rpm.

Land Rover 2.5-litre diesel FX4S
(1985 to 1987)
and FX4S-Plus
(1987 to 1988)

The Land Rover diesel was a development of the 2.3-litre diesel, with the principle changes being a bigger bore and a longer stroke, and the relocation of the injector pump drive to the front of the engine, via a toothed belt, enclosed in an alloy casing. The engine produced 69.6bhp at 4,000rpm.

Nissan TD27 2.7-litre diesel, Fairway
(early 1989 to early 1992),
Fairway Driver
(early 1992 to early 1995) and
Fairway 95
(early 1995 to Summer 1997)

The Nissan TD27 was a four-cylinder, in-line diesel of 2,663cc and produced 63.5Kw at 4,300rpm. It had a cast-iron block with integral crankcase, and the crank had five main bearings. The pistons had two compression rings and one oil control ring. The detachable cylinder head was cast iron, secured by bolts. It was of the Ricardo indirect injection type, with self-bleeding injectors and heater plugs. The valves were overhead, two per cylinder with the exhaust ports on the nearside and the

ABOVE More ancillaries were fitted to the Land Rover, and later variants, than to the Austin engine. These included the power-steering pump (with white filler cap). The fuel filter was bolted to one side of the radiator, which was larger than on previous models with pressurised cooling. *(Murray Jackson)*

BELOW The sheer bulk of the timing case of the 2.5 Land Rover diesel, seen on the front of the engine, made installation more difficult than with the 2.3-litre diesel. Although taken from the FX4S brochure, this image shows the original Land Rover transmission bolted to the back. *(London Taxi Company/London Vintage Taxi Association Archive)*

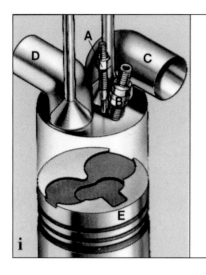

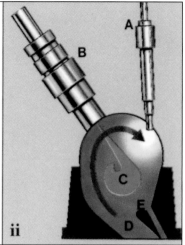

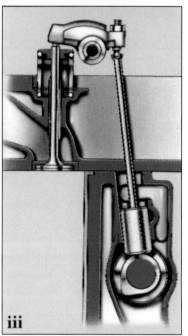

The Nissan TD27 diesel was a simple but extremely well-engineered engine. The cutaway views show: i) the crossflow design of the intake ports with A the vertically mounted glow plug, B, the injector nozzle, C, intake manifold, D, exhaust manifold and E the piston, with integral combustion chamber; ii) Combustion chamber, with auxiliary passage, showing A, the vertically mounted glow plug, B, the injector nozzle, C, injected fuel, D, main passage into cylinder; iii) high-mounted camshaft, which allowed for shorter pushrods and thus improved high-speed operation; iv) low-noise, high-meshing geartrain, showing gears for A, crankshaft, B, camshaft, C, idler D, fuel injector pump, E, oil pump.

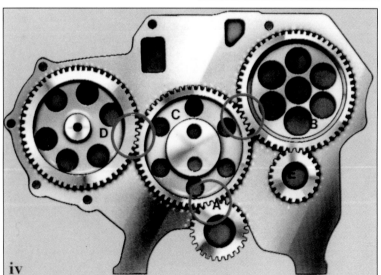

inlet ports on the offside. The timing chain and the injector pump were driven by gears from the front of engine. Lubrication was by gear-type pump with a full-flow filter and built-in oil cooler.

Transmissions

Automatic
Austin FX4
The original, and until 1961, the only transmission available was the Borg-Warner DG150M three-speed automatic. As well as a torque converter, it had a single-plate clutch that engaged when the transmission was in top gear, giving a direct drive to the torque converter output shaft.

The DG150M was replaced in 1964 with the Borg-Warner BW35 transmission. Although designed for engines of capacities between 1.5 and 2 litres, it was the only other transmission available to BMC, makers of the Austin diesel, which had a torque converter but not a lock-up clutch. The BW35 was offered until late 1980 when it was replaced with the BW65, which was a derivative of the BW35.

An automatic transmission was never offered for general sale with a petrol engine, although one single petrol automatic was made as a prototype for New York City in 1968.

The FX4R, FX4Q, FX4S and FX4S-Plus
A similar transmission to the BW65, the BW66 was fitted to the 2.3-litre Land Rover diesel and petrol engines in the FX4R. When Borg-Warner closed their UK factory in Letchworth, Hertfordshire, the Australian-made BW40 transmission was imported for the FX4S and S-Plus. The only transmission available on the FX4Q was the BW66. All these transmissions had floor-mounted selector levers.

Fairway and Fairway Driver
The Nissan Jatco RE4R01A automatic transmission, with three speeds plus overdrive, was fitted to the Nissan TD27 diesel in the Fairway and Fairway Driver. It had

vacuum and electronic gearchange control, a floor-mounted selector lever, and a push-button overdrive switch.

London Coach and London Sterling

These models came with just one transmission, the Ford C3 automatic with three speeds and low gear lock-up, cooled by a heavy duty oil cooler built into the radiator.

Manual

A manual transmission was not fitted to the Austin FX4 until 1962, when the gearbox used in the Austin Gipsy was adapted. This was offered until the last Austin taxi of Spring 1982 and on the small number of Carbodies FX4Ds made during that year. It had four forward speeds plus reverse, with synchromesh on second, third and top gears. The ratios, identical incidentally, to those of the Gypsy were: first, 4.05:1, second, 2.35:1, third, 1.37:1 top, 1:1 and reverse, 5.168:1. The clutch was a Borg & Beck single dry plate with coil springs, hydraulically operated, with a 10in (254mm) plate on the diesel model and a 9in (229mm) plate on the petrol model.

The manual transmission fitted to the Carbodies FX4R, FX4S and FX4S-Plus was a Rover five-speed plus reverse, with synchromesh on all forward gears and remote gearchange. Ratios were: first, 3.32:1, second, 2.087:1, third, 1.396:1, fourth, 1.00:1; top, 0.792:1 and reverse, 3.428:1. The clutch was a Borg & Beck single dry plate, hydraulically operated with a diaphragm spring and a 9.5in (240mm) plate. No manual transmission was offered on the FX4Q.

Fairway and Fairway Driver

The manual transmission fitted to the Fairway and Fairway Driver was a Nissan unit, with five forward speeds and reverse. Synchromesh was fitted to all forward speeds. Ratios were: first, 3.592:1, second, 2.246:1, third, 1.415:1, fourth, 1:1; top, 0.821:1 and reverse, 3.657:1. The clutch was hydraulically operated, with a single dry plate with a 240mm (9.4in) single plate and a diaphragm spring.

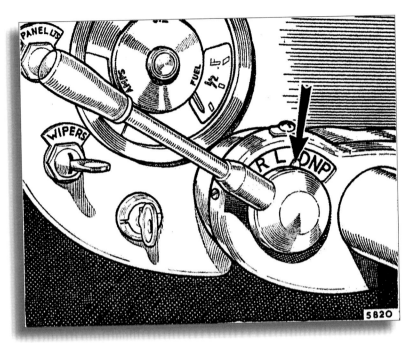

Cooling system

All engines fitted to FX4 models were water-cooled, with water pumps and thermostats. The first type of cooling system, fitted from 1958 to late 1971 in conjunction with the 2.2-litre Austin diesel, and from 1962 to 1972 with the 2.2-litre Austin petrol engine, used a water pump-assisted thermosyphon with an unpressurised radiator. The second type was fully pressurised, with an expansion tank mounted on the inner front wing. This was used with the 2.5-litre Austin diesel from late 1971 to late 1982, the 2.28 Land Rover diesel and petrol engines in the FX4R from 1982 to 1985,

ABOVE The gear selector for the automatic transmission on all Austin models except the FX4Q was mounted on the steering column. *(Author's Collection)*

BELOW The Austin manual gearbox, designed for the Austin Gipsy 4x4, was a robust and substantial unit. *(D.S. Taxis)*

and the 2.5-litre Land Rover diesel in the FX4S from 1985 to 1987. The third type was a larger pressurised radiator, used with the 2.5-litre Land Rover diesel in the FX4S-Plus from 1987 to 1988, and the Nissan TD27 diesel from 1989 to 1997. This radiator, when fitted to a cab with an automatic transmission, had a built-in transmission oil cooler. All engines were so fitted and the Nissan TD27 was equipped with a viscous fan.

Fuel systems – diesel

The fuel system of the 22E and 22K 2.2-litre Austin diesel engines fitted to the FX4D until 1971 consisted of an AC-Delco mechanical lift pump driven off the camshaft feeding the injector pump through a CAV filter. The first type of injector pump, fitted between 1958 and 1962, was a CAV-type BPE.4A in-line unit. A single Pinteaux injector fed each pre-combustion chamber. On this type of injector pump, the fuel supply was controlled by a vacuum created in the inlet manifold by a butterfly valve. In October 1962, the injector pump was changed to a DPA-type rotary pump. On this pump the fuel supply was controlled directly from the throttle pedal. Both pumps were mounted on the offside front of the engine, driven by a chain from

BELOW The fuel system on early diesel engines needed to be bled of air if the system was stripped or the vehicle had run out of fuel. This was done at the unions numbered.
(Author's Collection)

the crankshaft. The DPA pump was carried over to the 2.52-litre diesel and was used for the whole life of the engine, and on to the Kalaskai diesel fitted to the FX4Q.

Fuel supply to the pump was regulated by a stop control knob operated by the driver. From 1958 to Spring 1974, this knob was mounted below the dashboard, adjacent to the driver's left knee. From then, it was fitted to the steering column lock and could only be pushed into the 'on' position when the starter key was turned.

The CAV-type pump was also used on the Land Rover diesel engines: on the 2.3-litre engine it was mounted on the side of the block, where the distributor of the petrol engine would be mounted, and driven by a skew gear from the camshaft. On the FX4S and FX4S-Plus it was mounted on the nearside front, driven from the crankshaft by a toothed rubber belt. Both were fed from an AC-Delco mechanical lift pump. The stop control knob was again built into the steering lock, but was moved to the 'on' position by a spring when the starter key was turned. The 2.5-litre Land Rover diesel was fitted with a Micronova control system, whereby the fuel stop was controlled electrically by the starter switch. This system obviated the need for heater plugs, ensuring instant starting with no pre-heat. Both types of Land Rover engine had Pinteaux injectors.

Between 1976 and 1982, a glass agglomerator bowl, a water trap, was found on the fuel filter assembly. This was discontinued on FX4R diesel models, as a larger fuel filter was fitted, which had sufficient capacity to trap water without it contaminating the fuel.

The fuel tank was mounted at the rear of the vehicle, behind the rear axle and between the chassis side members. A gauze filter was fitted inside the tank, over the fuel outlet. The fuel filler tube was connected to an external ventilated filler cap, mounted on the nearside rear of the vehicle by a rubber flexible pipe. An overflow pipe extended from the top of the fuel filter housing to the offside of the tank.

The injector pump on the Nissan TD27 was a KI-KI, located on the front offside of

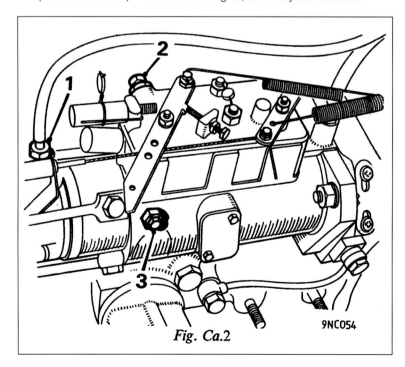

Fig. Ca.2   9NC054

the engine and driven from the same geartrain that drove the camshaft. It incorporated an integral lift pump.

Air cleaners

An oil bath air cleaner with a fabric venturi hose was used between 1958 and late 1971 on the diesel engine, and between 1958 and 1972 on the petrol engine. From 1971, various designs of cartridge air filter were used in pressed steel housings, depending on the engine, all with a plastic venturi hose.

Steering

A cam and lever-type steering box without power assistance was fitted to models made from 1958 to 1982, for a short time with a ratio of 20:1, later changed to 24:1. A 17in (430mm) Bakelite steering wheel was fitted. From May 1974, the steering column had a crash link to comply with European safety regulations. Power–assisted steering (PAS) was found on the FX4R and FL2 from 1982, originally as an option, but was standard from 1983. A smaller, 14in (355mm), two-spoke steering wheel was fitted to all models with PAS. Power assistance for the FX4R, FX4S, S-Plus, Fairway and Fairway Driver steering was provided by a pump, mounted on the offside front of the engine and driven by a belt. The crash link on Fairway Driver and Fairway 95 models was of a different pattern from earlier types.

Axles, suspension, wheels and tyres

Front suspension

Two types of independent front suspension were found on the FX4 and one on the FL2, the first being the original BMC pattern, used on all FL2s and on FX4s between 1958 and February 1992, and the completely new type, introduced on the Fairway Driver in February 1992. The original type consisted of a coil spring bearing each side of a lower wishbone, which were held to the detachable front axle beam on wishbone rubbers. An Armstrong lever arm shock absorber acted as the upper

ABOVE The fuel filter fitted to the Austin 2.5-litre diesel and all subsequent engines was of a canister type. Note the twin plastic brake fluid reservoirs, fitted between 1969 and 1982. *(Author)*

BELOW The manual steering box, fitted to all Austin and early Carbodies models. Later types, from Spring 1974, had a crash link fitted to the column. *(Author)*

wishbone. The upper and lower wishbones were each connected to a kingpin and stub axle assembly by fulcrum pins.

The Fairway Driver type consisted of upper and lower wishbones each side, with a concentric coil spring and a telescopic shock absorber bearing on the lower wishbone. Each wishbone was attached to an upright with a stub axle. As with the original type, the wishbones were mounted on the detachable axle beam by rubber bushes.

Rear axle and suspension

A live beam rear axle mounted on leaf springs was used on all models. From 1958 to February 1992, a hypoid, three-quarter-floating Salisbury axle was fitted, with different ratios according to the model. On models built from 1958 to September 1987, the axle was hung on nine-leaf semi-elliptical steel leaf springs (ten-leaf on certain provincial models), with lever-arm shock absorbers. On the FX4S-Plus models, introduced in February 1987, GKN Literide carbon fibre single-leaf springs were used, with telescopic shock absorbers. Literide springs were also fitted to the Fairway, introduced in February 1989, and

on the earliest of the Fairway Driver models from February 1992. Subsequent Fairway Driver and Fairway 95 models were fitted with single-leaf steel springs, with a helper spring, with telescopic shock absorbers. All Fairway Driver and Fairway 95 models had a GKN fully floating hypoid rear axle.

Two types of wheel, both steel disc, were found on the FX4. Up to Spring 1992, a 16in x 4J type with five studs was fitted. From spring 1992, a deeply dished wheel was fitted, again 16in, but with 5J rims.

Tyres

The first type of tyre fitted as standard, and used until the early 1980s, was the Dunlop Super Taxicord crossply tubeless. The size fitted to the taxi was 5.75-16, six-ply, and 6.00-16 six-ply tyres were supplied with the FL2. Recommended pressures were 28psi all round. Michelin X radial-ply taxi tyres were also available. From the early 1980s until 1997, 175-16 Dunlop Super Taxi radial ply tyres became standard fitting from new, with Michelin ZX available as well as various remoulds for older cabs. Recommended pressure for radial tyres was 35psi all round.

RIGHT The front suspension and steering fitted to all FX4s up to 1992 was a standard BMC pattern, with kingpins and fulcrum pins and an armstrong lever arm shock absorber acting as the upper wishbone.
(D.S. Taxis)

Brakes

Two types of brake system were found on FX4 models, both with dual-circuit hydraulic operation on all four wheels. A mechanical handbrake operated on the rear wheels. The first, used from 1958 to early 1992, had 11in (280mm) drums all round. The drum brake arrangement had twin leading shoes on the front and single leading shoes on the rear. Front and rear brakes were adjusted manually. On all models built between 1958 and September 1982, the pedal assembly was mounted on a shaft under the floor, originally acting on twin hydraulic master cylinders. From 1958 to 1969, the fluid reservoir, found under the bonnet was a single steel canister with two compartments divided concentrically. Subsequently, two single plastic reservoirs were fitted. From 1976 to September 1982, servo assistance was fitted to the front wheels only. The servo was fitted under the bonnet, on the scuttle adjacent to the steering column, with a single, divided plastic fluid reservoir. Vacuum was provided by a pump, mounted on a fabricated steel bracket bolted to the nearside of the cylinder head, and driven by its own V-belt.

On all models from September 1982 to February 1989, the pedal arrangement was a pendant setup with servo assistance on all four wheels, with a tandem dual circuit master cylinder mounted in front of the servo. The servo pump arrangement introduced in 1976 was carried over to the FX4R and FL2 London Limousine, but was replaced on the FX4S and FX4S-Plus by a pump driven from the camshaft, located where the injector pump would be on the 2.3-litre diesel engine. The servo pump for all Fairway models was mounted on the back of the alternator and thus driven by the same drive belt. Larger wheel cylinders were fitted on all models made between September 1982 and February 1992. An aftermarket disc brake conversion for the front axle, manufactured by Zeus, was offered from 1991 for all models that had full servo assistance.

From 1992, on all Fairway Driver and Fairway 95 models, a completely different design of brake was used. Ventilated discs with four-pot callipers were fitted on the front, with 10in (254mm) drums with self-adjusting shoes on the rear. The pedal, servo and reservoir arrangement was the same as on the original Fairway.

On all models, the handbrake was operated by a centrally mounted pull-up lever, acting on the rear wheels. On all models up to the introduction of the Fairway Driver in February 1992, the lever acted through a system of rods and bell cranks. The lever fitted from 1958 to 1970 was a chromium-plated type, while all subsequent models had a black, pressed steel type. On the Fairway Driver and Fairway 95, the handbrake operated via a cable attached to a centrally mounted pull-up lever.

Electrical system

The electrical system on all models was 12V. From 1958 to late 1971 it was positive earth, with power generated by a dynamo. All Austin petrol models had positive earth, with dynamos. Taxis built from late 1971, with 2.52-litre 25V diesel and all subsequent models, had negative earth and

BELOW **Drum brakes were fitted to all FX4s until early 1992. The design remained basically the same, with the exception of the fitting of larger wheel cylinders in 1982. This shows the front brakes, which had twin leading shoes.** (D.S. Taxis)

RIGHT The limpet or 'bunny ear' indicators were a distinctive feature of early FX4s, and much despised. *(Author)*

an alternator was fitted. Fuse boxes on all models up to the FX4S were fitted under the bonnet. Fuses for the FX4S-Plus and all Fairway models were located under the dash, close to the driver's door in a pull-down box.

All 2.2-litre diesel models were originally fitted with two 138-amp/hr 6V batteries, wired in series and mounted, one over each wheel arch. All subsequent models were fitted with a single, 95-amp/hr 12V battery, mounted on the nearside wheel arch. The starter motor on all engines was a pre-engaged type.

RIGHT The revised taillights were a far better arrangement than the original types. They were borrowed from the MkII BMC 1100/1300 range, and Lucas, the manufacturer, continued to make them for 23 years after that car went out of production. *(Author)*

Lights and electrical ancillaries

Two headlights, one mounted in each of the front wings, were fitted to all models. Between 1958 and 1967 these were of a bulb and reflector type and the front sidelights were mounted on top of the wings. Models built between 1968 and early 1989 had sealed-beam headlight units, with sidelights incorporated in the unit with separate, capless bulbs. Fairway models, built from 1989, had separate halogen headlight bulbs with a dim-dip facility. The sidelights were integral with the headlight units, and had separate bulbs. Tail lights on all models built before 1969 had combined stop and tail light bulbs behind a triangular red lens, and were fitted with an inbuilt reflector. From 1969, these were changed to a combination unit, housing stop and tail lights behind a red section of the two-part lens, with the indicator bulb behind the upper, amber lens, and the combined stop/tail light with a double filament bulb behind the lower, red lens. A separate red reflector was placed on the red lens.

Indicators on FX4s built up to 1969 were the 'limpet', roof-mounted type. FL2 Hire Cars built from about 1964 did not have limpet indicators, but were fitted with amber circular indicators, mounted on the front and rear wings. On the FX4, from 1969, separate orange front indicator lights, of a similar pattern to those adopted for the FL2, were fitted, along with a small rectangular repeater indicators mounted on the front wings.

A single fog lamp was originally supplied, but this later became an optional extra. Separate halogen fog lamps were offered as optional extras from around 1980. A number plate light was fitted to all models, with a single bulb under a shroud. Until about 1989, this shroud was of pressed steel, but subsequently of plastic. The original mounting was below the number plate, and on early FL2 models, the plate was hinged at the top so as to hang vertically when the boot was fully open. This was changed on all models in the latter half of the 1960s to a fitting above the number plate. The number plate was then fixed directly to the boot lid.

Reversing lights, offered as an optional extra from 1975, were rectangular and were operated by a non-self-cancelling pull switch. A telltale white light was embedded in the end of the switch. From 1980, these were replaced by a square type, but still mounted on the rear panel. On the FX4R and subsequent models, all of which had an integral reversing light switch on both manual and automatic transmissions, the reversing lights were operated when reverse gear was engaged. Reversing lights fitted from the FX4R onwards were of a separate type, hung below the rear bumper. Rear fog lights, of a similar construction to the separate reversing lights, were optional extras on base FL models from 1980. They were fitted as standard equipment on some subsequent higher-specification models and all Fairway Drivers and Fairway 95s. A high-level brake light was fitted as standard on the FX4S-Plus. This was the first British vehicle to be offered with this feature.

Windscreen wipers on all models were driven by a single Lucas electric motor, located on the nearside of the scuttle, driving through a rack and wheelboxes. Two-speed wipers were fitted from 1980, and an intermittent wipe facility with electric screen wash from 1985 on the FX4S.

Interior fittings and trim

The original Austin FX4D
(1958 to 1969) and FX4 (1962 to 1969)

The passenger compartment of the FX4D and FX4 was trimmed with pleated dark tan leather seat facings and similar colour Rexine on the seat edges, the rear armrests, the back rests and bases for the tip-up seats and the panels between and either side of them. The door and inner wing panels were plastic mouldings of a similar colour. In the first two years or so of production, the paint around the inside of all external windows was body colour (almost exclusively black), but was changed to a light tan colour, similar to that of the demonstration model, VLW 431. The rearward-facing tip-up seats had springs to return them to the upright position when not in use. The headlining was of light tan vinyl. The floor, the lower edge of the partition, and the vertical face below the rear seat cushion were covered in brown rubber matting that had a small square pattern. The panels covering the forward interior edge of the wheel arches were pressed from alloy sheet

and featured a square pattern. The step treads were a ribbed alloy casting.

Two courtesy lights were fitted in the roof above the rear passenger seats and were operated by a push-button switch, mounted on the inside of the nearside C-post. A chromium-plated handle was fixed to the inside of each door and two light tan soft plastic handles were fitted, one vertically and at an angle to the C-post, and adjacent to the rear side window. The door was opened by a chromium-plated lever, situated close to the forward edge of each door and held by a leather check strap. The

ABOVE These early tip-up seats were trimmed with leather. The fare table was fixed in the glass frame, set between the seats. *(Author)*

LEFT The trim of early FX4s was brown in colour. The solid-looking handle for opening the door was a replacement for the original which, like the exterior handles, was not strong enough for the job. The earliest models had body-colour paint around the doors and windows, changed later, until 1967, to the light tan colour shown here. *(Author)*

windows were of a constant-balance type, held on a spring, with the movement dampened by felt-covered rubber channels. They were pulled up or down by an almost full-width alloy casting, fixed to the top edge of the glass.

A recirculating heater was mounted under the rear passenger seat, with a fan controlled by a single chromium-plated toggle switch, mounted on the offside C-post. A partition divided the driver and passenger compartments, with safety glass in the upper part, divided into two by a vertical support. Originally, a circular panel was fitted in the centre of the driver's side glass, with a rotating part to either allow speech or privacy. This was found to be ineffective and was replaced in April 1960 by a vertically sliding panel in the centre of the partition.

A single chromium-plated circular ashtray was fitted in each door. The fare table was held in a brown painted frame, covered by glass. The small PCO plate bearing the licence number was screwed below it with a white plastic sign bearing the words 'The number of this cab is'. Above the fare table was a small, white rectangular plate with the message 'Please sit well back in your seat for safety and comfort'. A circular badge with the Austin coat of arms was fitted on early models to the panel above the partition glass. In 1967, the seat facings were changed to vinyl and the paint around the window frames was changed to body colour.

The original Austin FL2D
(1958 to late 1969) and FL2 (October 1962 to late 1969)
The standard of equipment fitted in the rear of the FL2 and FL2D was the same as the FX4 and FX4D, except for the partition and the occasional seats, and the use of interior rear door handles identical to the ones used on the taxi. The partition was angled back and housed two forward-facing seats that folded out. The partition glass consisted of two panes, the offside one sliding horizontally to allow contact with the driver. A third ashtray and two more soft grab handles were fixed to the partition.

The revised Austin FX4 and FX4D
The fixtures, fittings and level of trim of the facelifted model were based on the preceding model, but with several differences. The colour of the trim was changed to black and

RIGHT Although the trim of the early FX4 and FL2 shared many common components, there were some detail differences. One was the interior door handle, originally used on the taxi but discarded as it was too fragile, and the trim panel. The wide alloy window pulls were changed to a narrower design on both taxi and Hire Car in 1969. *(Author)*

FAR RIGHT The biggest difference between the FL2 and the FX4 was in the occasional seats. As can be seen, the FL2's fold out from the partition and faced forward. Note also the grab handles and ash tray mounted on the partition. *(Author)*

RIGHT On the 'new shape', most of the interior retained the same design, although the trim colour was changed to black and the mat was now grey. The paint around the windows was changed from light tan to body colour in 1967. *(Murray Jackson)*

the colour of the rubber floor matting was changed to grey. The angled-back partition, borrowed from the FL2, was fitted with the same vertical glass panes, but with the opening of the sliding part restricted by the Conditions of Fitness to four inches. The passenger compartment heater was relocated to between the tip-up seats, drawing air through a circular grille and discharging it through two rectangular grilles above and below. Although still rearward-facing, the tip-up seats were of a different type from the original FX4, having an external steel frame with the seat cushions screwed to a plywood base fitted into them. The fare table remained in its original position but was covered by a single hard plastic sheet with no frame. The headlining was changed to one with a black and white fine-striped 'tiger' pattern.

On models built from Spring 1974, the rear seat cushion was changed to one with a high front roll to ensure passengers sat well back in their seats, as a sign that had been fitted to the bulkhead since 1958 had urged them to do, with the main part of the seat having wider pleats than before. The door handles were relocated to the centre of the door, underneath a long, flexible grab handle. From 1976, window locks, each comprising a lever pivoted on a vertical pin that slid under the fully raised glass,

FAR LEFT The interior was further revised in 1974 to comply with the new European safety laws. The rear seat was reprofiled and, to suit the new burst-proof door locks, the interior door handles were moved to the centre of the doors. This interior was carried over to the FX4R and, as shown here, the FX4Q. *(Author)*

LEFT From 1974, the passenger side of the partition received a makeover, with the centre part redesigned. The heater remained in place. The adverts on the tip-up seats also served to keep the seat backs clean. *(Author)*

were fitted and from 1978 there were clear plastic guards over the interior door handles. The ashtrays, while remaining in the doors, were changed from chromium-plated steel to Stelvitite (plastic-coated steel).

The revised Austin FL2 and FL2D

The interior of the facelifted FL2 and FL2D was trimmed in identical material to the FX4 and FX4D, although the partition and the original forward-facing occasional seats remained.

FX4R and FX4S

The interior of the FX4R and the FX4S was similar to the previous Carbodies FX4D, but with a few small differences. Motion locks were fitted to all doors from October 1983, which prevented the doors from being opened when the cab was driven faster than walking pace and, when the footbrake pedal was depressed, a small red light fitted just above the door handle illuminated to show the passengers when the lock was operative. On the FX4S, seat belts for passengers in the rear seats were fitted, with the reels mounted on top of the parcel shelf. Moulded plastic draught excluders were fitted to the door sills

and draught-proofing strips were fitted to the bottom of the doors.

FX4S-Plus, Fairway, Fairway Driver and Fairway 95

The interior of the FX4S-Plus was completely revised. It became a full five-seater with new, completely re-profiled trim panels in moulded grey plastic and new grey seats in plastic or optional velour. The headlining was changed to a light-coloured plastic with a fine tweed pattern print. The grab handles were red plastic to aid the visually impaired. Two ashtrays were fitted adjacent to the rear armrest and the controls for the two-speed heater fan, one for speed and one on-off switch were mounted on the fascia. Four courtesy lights were fitted: two in the original position and two at low level in the front of the panel that covers the wheel arch, to illuminate the doorway.

The interior of the first Fairway model was based on the FX4S-Plus, but with wheelchair accommodation. This facility was created by dog-legging the partition into the luggage platform. The heater outlet was moved to below the offside tip-up seat and the heater controls were located on the angled part of the partition. The rear seat cushion lifted up to allow a wheelchair to be manoeuvred into a rearwards-facing position. At the bottom of the partition, a lockable belt on an inertia reel, was fitted to allow a hook that located on the wheelchair frame to secure it in place. The lock was electrically operated and was controlled by an illuminated switch on the facia, adjacent to the nearside passenger door. An inertia-reel seatbelt, with a short extension piece where needed, could secure the wheelchair passenger in place.

Three trim levels were offered on the Fairway: Bronze, Silver and Gold. The Fairway Driver continued with the same trim options. The Fairway Driver Plus featured a rear seat cushion that was split 50/50, so that a wheelchair with slightly longer footrests could be accommodated with the nearside half of the seat cushion raised, and a passenger could still sit on the lowered half of the seat. The Fairway 95 came with a single standard of trim, with carpets in the passenger compartment as standard. A new trim material, with a pattern on

BELOW **The FX4S-Plus and early Fairway shared the same design of interior. This is from a Silver model, although the headrests, a standard fitting on the Gold model, have been fitted as an extra.**
(Ceejay Autos)

the centre panels was used, and red sections were included on the front of the rear seats to aid the visually impaired.

FL2 London Limousine

On the London Limousine a wide variety of extras, including leather seats, wood door cappings and cocktail cabinets were available, and each model was trimmed according to the requirements of the customer. Aside from that, the basic fittings, such as door handles and windows, were the same as the FX4R.

The London Coach and London Sterling

Although a taxi, the London Coach was fitted out with rather better trim than the standard FX4S, upon which it was based. All interior panels and seats were deep-padded and trimmed in vinyl and the floor was carpeted. In the London Sterling, being a limousine, the passenger compartment was even better finished, with many luxury items as standard including a rear centre console finished in walnut, an AM/FM stereo radio/cassette player with four speakers, electric windows, digital quartz clock, air conditioning, leather covering to the upper door panels, velour trim, folding armrest in the rear seat, and a cigar lighter.

Driver's compartment and instrumentation and luggage platform

The original Austin FX4 and FX4D

The instruments were housed in a panel in front of the driver. The first design contained two dials: a speedometer on the right with a built-in fuel gauge, incorporating the blue main beam and red dynamo warning lamps,

ABOVE The London Coach interior was far more sumptuous than the equivalent British model, the FX4S.
(Don Smith)

FAR LEFT The first design of partition used this circular aperture, which proved useless and was replaced by a vertically sliding glass panel. The small white sign reads 'Please sit well back in your seat for safety and comfort'.
(Author)

LEFT The driver's accommodation in the earliest FX4 was basic, bordering on crude by today's standards. At least in 1958 he had the luxury of a fourth door for the first time. The instruments were comprehensive in comparison with contemporary cars.
(Author)

FX4W and other wheelchair conversions

BELOW The CR6 was tested as a wheelchair-carrying vehicle and much was learned from this exercise, especially that there were a lot of people in wheelchairs who desperately wanted greater mobility. Intended to be fitted to existing cabs, the FX4W conversion provided that facility. This early prototype has the door hinged on the B-post for easier access. *(London Taxi Company/ London Vintage Taxi Association Archive)*

"Start with taxis!" This was the clear message given by wheelchair-bound people, when the Department of Transport interviewed them about transport issues during the International Year of the Disabled in 1981. "The pavements are so bad, we struggle to get anywhere in the first place!" Thus the DoT, through tireless civil servant and campaigner for disabled people, Ann Frye began work on making purpose-built taxis wheelchair-accessible, which gelled in the form of two deadlines: one in 1989, when all new purpose-built taxis had to be wheelchair-accessible, and 1 January 2000, when all purpose-built taxis in the UK had to be wheelchair-accessible.

Introduced in March 1986, the FX4W conversion was a full wheelchair-accessible conversion for new or existing FX4s. It was developed by Roger Ponticelli of Carbodies Sales & Service Ltd, and consisted of a divided partition, with the nearside part sliding forward to make space for the wheelchair, a lifting rear-seat cushion, full securing devices and 180° nearside rear-door opening facility. It was exhibited at the 1987 Mobility Roadshow, and shown to HRH The Princess Royal by Andrew Overton. A later version with a fixed partition and a door that opened 180° against the back wing was offered at a lower price of £995. This was discontinued in 1989 with the introduction of Fairway, which had wheelchair accessibility built in. When wheelchair accessibility became mandatory for purpose-built taxis in 2000, a number of specialist conversions became available to enable proprietors to keep their cabs on the road for a few more years. These conversions cost in the region of £1,500. The TX1 was the first purpose-built cab produced by LTI that had wheelchair accessibility built in from its initial design stages.

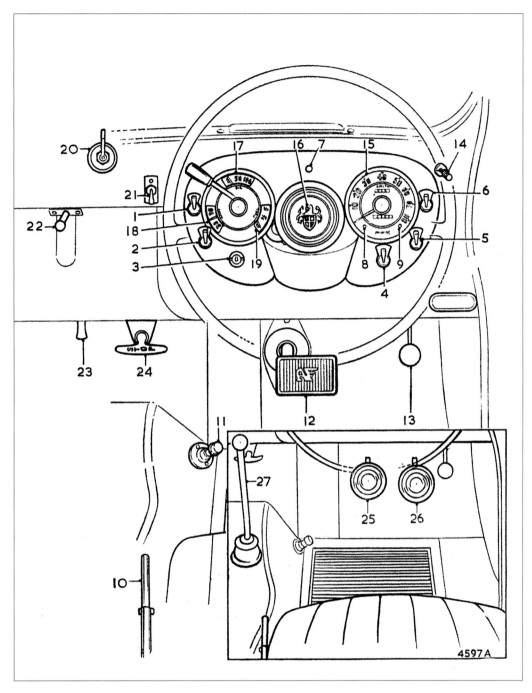

LEFT Controls and instruments. (London Taxi Company/Author's Collection)

1 Panel lamp switch
2 Wiper switch
3 Master switch
4 Main lighting switch
5 Interior lamp switch
6 Fog lamp switch
7 Direction indicator warning light
8 Main-beam warning lamp
9 Dynamo warning lamp
10 Handbrake
11 Headlamp dipper switch
12 Brake pedal (Automatic gearbox)
13 Accelerator pedal
14 Speedometer trip control
15 Speedometer
16 Horn-push
17 Oil gauge
18 Ammeter
19 Fuel gauge
20 Direction indicator switch
21 Heater switch
22 Ventilator control
23 Heater door control
24 Engine stop control
25 Clutch pedal (Synchromesh gearbox)
26 Brake pedal (Synchromesh gearbox)
27 Gear change lever (Synchromesh gearbox)

and a composite instrument with oil pressure and fuel gauges, ammeter, charging light and indicator warning light, on the left. The original position of the indicator warning light was in the centre of the instrument panel, but on later models it was found on the windscreen frame, near the vacuum-controlled self-cancelling indicator switch.

From November 1960 a three-piece instrument panel was fitted, with the left-hand composite instrument containing the fuel gauge, oil pressure gauge and ammeter, and a separate water temperature gauge fitted in a small, centrally mounted steel plate. The speedometer with the same warning lights incorporated remained unchanged. A starter switch, combining the switch for the heater plugs, was fitted to the lower part of the instrument panel, to the driver's left. Current to the wipers, indicators and stoplights was carried through this switch. Lucas toggle switches on the instrument panel operated the headlights and sidelights, wipers, rear heater fan motor (with a facility to override the passenger's switch), the rear fog lights and the passenger compartment interior light (also with a facility to override the passenger's switch). The driver's heater fan switch was fixed to the windscreen frame pressing, to the left of the instrument panel.

Two orange lamps, which lit up when either of the passenger doors was not fully closed, were located above the windscreen in front of the driver. A black fibreboard panel extended below the dashboard, with a smaller, separate access panel below the instrument panel. The zero control for the trip meter was fitted on the steel cowl of the dash, close to the windscreen upright. A small chromium-plated ashtray, swivelling on a vertical axis, was fitted adjacent to the driver's right knee. The driver's seat was faced with brown leather and had a matching Rexine side trim and was adjustable forward and aft, and for height.

The column gearchange lever for the automatic gearbox was housed in a pressed steel binnacle. It had a white indicator panel with black letters, illuminated from behind. The gear lever for the manual gearbox was centrally placed. The brake pedal and, where fitted, the clutch pedal were circular. The accelerator pedal was circular on all models. The chromium-plated pull-up type handbrake lever was also centrally mounted. The steering wheel was two-spoke, black Bakelite with, originally, a painted alloy centre horn push, but from 1965 with a chromium-plated trim ring and the Austin coat of arms contained in plastic.

The headlight dipswitch was mounted on the floor, adjacent to the driver's left foot. The engine stop control knob was mounted under the dashboard adjacent to the driver's left knee and was the only way of turning off the engine. A single, Rexine-covered sun visor was provided for the driver and a single courtesy light was fitted above and behind the driver, on the partition, operated by a chromium-plated toggle switch to the side of it. Each front door was opened from the inside by a single chromium-plated handle, located at the forward edge. (This was one of the very few items that would remain the same throughout the cab's production life.) A single chromium-plated pull

handle was fixed to the inside of the driver's door and a cord check strap was secured at one end to the bottom of the dashboard and at the other end to the luggage platform door, to enable the driver to close the door without moving from his seat. Both front doors had a thick leather check strap. The floor had a thick black rubber mat and the sills were covered by a bright alloy pressing with an embossed, square pattern. From March 1963, front-seat belt anchorages were fitted and from 1966, a fixed-type lap-and-diagonal seat belt was provided for the driver. In 1967, the facing of the driver's seat was changed from leather to vinyl.

A pressed steel partition separated the driver's compartment from the luggage platform and had a padded armrest. The luggage platform was covered by a thick rubber mat with alloy coverings to the door side of a type similar to those on the driver's side. A horizontal steel rail was screwed to the partition, which served as anchorage for a leather strap, provided to secure the luggage. The paintwork around the door windows was body colour. Until 1967, Bakelite mouldings covered the inside of the windscreen pillars. A handle to open the scuttle vent was located just above it, with a Bakelite knob.

Air from the driver's heater was controlled by a spring-loaded flap, under the centre of the dashboard, directing it either to the floor when lowered, or to the windscreen when raised, through two narrow slits when closed. Pushing it to the closed position directed air to the windscreen demister vents. Bright alloy shields directed air further to the windscreen. The taximeter was mounted on a bracket, which was bolted to the inner face of the B-post and was switched on and off by a single toggle switch located on the partition above the glass. Access to the bulb in the roof light was by a circular plate, held in place by a flat steel spring. The sign was lit by one single-filament bulb. This light was lit when the meter was switched on and set to 'For Hire', and extinguished when the meter was set to 'Hired' or 'Stopped', or was turned off. On cabs sold by London dealer Mann & Overton, a commission plate was fitted to the partition below the meter, giving the date of commission of the taxi, and its chassis number.

The original Austin FL2D

(1958 to 1969) and FL2
(October 1962 to 1969)

The driver's compartment of the Hire Car was fitted out in the same way as the taxi, except that an extra front bucket seat for a passenger and twin sun visors were fitted. There was no commission plate. Hire Cars were not sold exclusively by Mann & Overton and there was neither a taximeter nor the fittings for one.

The facelifted Austin FX4 and FX4D

The instrument panel and controls were virtually unchanged, the exception being from 1970 a different handbrake lever of black-painted pressed steel instead of a chromium-plated forging. The driver's seat frame was of a different design and could be adjusted for rake as well as height. On the automatic transmission model, the single brake pedal was rectangular. The covering for the seat was changed back to leather from 1969 after complaints about the vinyl causing excessive perspiration. An interior rear-view mirror was fitted, originally to the top of the dashboard, but from Spring 1974 it was hung from the top of the windscreen frame. The luggage strap was changed in 1971 from leather to rubberised webbing, and from 1974 the chromium-plated pull handle on the driver's door was replaced by a soft plastic handle.

The FX4D and FL2D from 1974, FX4R, FL2 London Limousine, FX4Q, FX4S and London Coach

In Spring 1974, the instrument panel was changed with the dials placed in a rectangular Stelvetite panel of a similar size to the original, with a plastic sun shield. The two orange warning lights for the doors and the single green warning light for the indicators were placed on the instrument panel. A red translucent pull switch for the hazard warning lights was situated on the bottom right of the instrument panel, with a built-in warning light. The indicators were operated by a self-cancelling stalk on the steering column, which also incorporated the horn push and headlight flasher. The two-spoke steering wheel was made of a softer plastic, with an energy-absorbing bush in the centre bearing the

Leyland symbol. A steering lock and combined engine stop switch were fitted.

From 1976, the brass tap on the cylinder head controlling the hot water supply for the heater was replaced by a slide control, located in the lower part of the centre of the dashboard. A low brake fluid warning light with built-in bulb tester was fitted to the instrument panel. From 1980, personal radios were allowed and were fitted over the aperture that gave access for the

ABOVE **The instrument panel and controls were revised in the Spring of 1974. This design, with minor modifications to the switchgear, lasted until the arrival of the FX4S-Plus in 1987.**
(Author)

'Taxi' sign bulb. This was an optional extra and by no means fitted to all cabs at the time. Just one single, low-power speaker was allowed, located in the binnacle.

The driver's compartment of the FX4R was basically similar to the preceding Austin and Carbodies models, but was fitted with an armrest for the driver, mounted on the door. From 1983, a red warning light for the motion locks, which lit up when the locks were operative, was located on the instrument panel. On earlier models without power steering, the Austin steering wheel was carried over, but the power steering models were fitted with a smaller, two-spoke wheel. Where the engine stop switch on the Austin and Carbodies FX4D had to be pushed in manually to allow fuel to the engine, the FX4R's was spring loaded, and activated when the key was turned. It had to be pulled out manually to stop the engine. The Micronova starting system on the FX4S did away with the stop knob.

On the FX4S, the switches on the instrument panel were of the rocker type. Two levers, taken from current Austin-Rover models were fitted to the steering column, the left-hand one for the indicators, horn and headlight dipswitch, the right-hand one for the wiper controls and electric screen washer. A new two-spoke steering wheel was fitted with the LTI logo in the centre. Moulded plastic draught excluders were fitted to the door sills and a draught-proofing strip fitted to the bottom of the doors.

The London Coach and London Sterling had the same instrumentation as the FX4S, but of course all situated for left-hand drive. The trim was of a much higher standard, with the same padded door trims, incorporating an elasticated map pocket, a centre console for the driver's air conditioning, and a second front seat.

FX4S-Plus, Fairway and Fairway Driver

For the FX4S-Plus, the driver's compartment and luggage platform received a major change, to match the rest of the interior. It featured a completely new moulded dashboard in grey plastic, with the instrument panel from the Austin Metro. Another new design of two-spoke steering wheel was fitted. This incorporated two dials, with the speedometer, odometer and trip meter on the right and the fuel gauge and water temperature gauge on the left. Between the two there was a panel of warning lights, incorporating those for indicators, main beam, sidelights, brake fluid level, handbrake operation, motion lock operation, low oil pressure, windscreen washer low level, battery charge, and open left- and right-hand doors.

Six push-button switches were located in a central panel. Five were functional, operating the rear interior lights, the driver's compartment light, the hazard warning lights, the rear fog lamp and the heated rear screen, with one spare, blanked-off switch. This was often replaced by a rocker switch operating the intercom. Two rocker switches were located adjacent to the driver's left knee. The left-hand one was set aside as an on-off switch for the taximeter (which was rarely used, as the meters had such a switch built in), and the right-hand for high- or low-level instrument lights.

The headlights and sidelights were operated from a switch on the left-hand side of the steering column. Indicators and wipers were operated in the same way as those of the FX4S. Fresh air vents were provided at the extreme ends of the dashboard and acted also as side window demisters. The heater controls, which were located in the central panel below the square switches consisted of two rocker switches, one each for the two-speed front and rear heater fans, as well as two slide controls, one for heat and one for the direction of air flow. Also housed in the same panel was the cigar lighter. A slot was provided in the lower part of the central binnacle for a radio and two housings for speakers were located at the extreme lower ends of the dash. A cubbyhole was provided at the opposite end of the dash from the instrument panel.

A binnacle fitted over the aperture for the 'Taxi' sign housed the controls for the electrically adjustable door mirrors, a digital clock, a courtesy light operated by switches in the doors, and an optional mounting for the taximeter. A centrally mounted console provided a combined locking box with a padded armrest built on the lid. On the front face was the operating switch for the electric platform door window fitted to the HLS model. There was a central receptacle, larger on the automatic models and smaller on the manual models. Forward of this was either the gearchange lever for the manual transmission models or, slightly further forward, the lever for the automatic gearchange. In a separate housing at the front of the centre console was an ashtray and the override for the fuel cut-off switch.

Almost all these features were carried over to the Fairway, with the addition of three extra warning lights on the dashboard, above the driver's side air vent. These consisted of a red light for when the fuel filter needed changing, an amber light to show when the heater plugs were warming, and a green light, fitted to automatic models, which came on when the overdrive gear was disengaged. Located on the forward part of the centre console were a rocker switch to operate the central locking and a push-button switch to engage fourth gear on automatic models, plus two blanks for switches to operate electric windows in the passenger doors. Because the gearbox was different, the gear lever for the manual gearbox was located

in a slightly different position. The lever was longer and stouter. On the Silver and Gold models of early Fairways, and on later Fairways, there were two switches for both electric front windows on the front face of the housing for the locker/armrest.

The opening part of the centre partition glass in the first Fairway model was located behind the driver, but on the Fairway Driver and Fairway 95, it was positioned above the luggage platform. The Fairway Driver Plus was fitted with a payment hatch in the angled part of the partition, but this created a draught around the driver's neck and subsequently, most, if not all, were replaced with the sliding partition from the original Fairway Driver.

ABOVE The Fairway inherited the dashboard of the FX4S-Plus, with the minor detail change of three warning lights close to the door. *(London Vintage Taxi Association Archive)*

BELOW A roof binnacle was fitted to the FX4S-Plus and all Fairway models. Covering the access panel for the roof sign, it housed, on the S-plus a clock, and on the Fairway series, the switch for the electrically adjusted door mirrors, a clock and, optionally, the taximeter. *(London Taxi Company/London Vintage Taxi Association Archive)*

RIGHT This illustration – from an FL2 brochure – shows the twin batteries, the absence of soundproofing and, airbrushed in alongside the original fragile steel rod bonnet prop, the more substantial telescopic one that was used until 1979. *(Author's Collection)*

RIGHT The single battery, pressurised radiator, twin plastic brake fluid reservoirs and water trap under the fuel filter are all visible in this 1970s brochure image. *(London Taxi Company/ London Vintage Taxi Association Archive)*

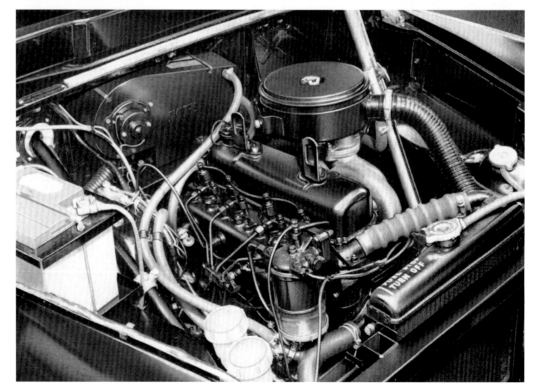

Under-bonnet fittings

The original Austin FX4 and FX4D

The bonnet pressing was braced by a substantial tubular steel X-member. The bonnet prop was of a telescopic type, fixed to the nearside chassis rail. A 6V battery was fitted on each of the inner wing panels. The scuttle had indentations for the steering column on both sides, to accommodate the installation of both left-hand and right-hand drive controls. A brass tap for the hot water control for front and rear heaters was located at the rear of the cylinder head. The bonnet release knob was placed on the front valance, and the safety release lever was mounted on the cross-member. A brass tap was incorporated into the fuel pipe, which acted as an emergency fuel stop. A small plate fixed to the valance advised of its location.

The revised Austin FX4, FX4D FL2 and FL2D

The revised model had a soundproofing pad placed between the X-brace and the bonnet pressing. The inner wings were re-profiled to accommodate a rain channel. The bonnet release mechanism consisted of two levers protruding from the front of the bonnet, the offside one operating the actual release and the nearside one the safety catch.

From late 1971, with the introduction of the 2.52-litre engine, a single 12V battery was fitted on the nearside inner wing. As the twin 6V batteries on earlier models came to the end of their lives, they were replaced by single 12V batteries. A steel rod bonnet prop was fitted in place of the telescopic type from late 1979.

The FX4R, FX4S, FX4S-Plus, London Coach and all Fairway models

The major difference in equipment under the bonnet of these models, engine notwithstanding, was the siting of a rectangular steel box, located against the scuttle that mounted the pendant pedals, the master cylinders and the brake servo. A safety switch to cut off the fuel supply in an emergency was mounted on the top of this

Chassis number codes

Austin, and subsequently Carbodies, gave each of the different FX4 models their own specific codes, depending on the engine and the manufacturer, which were used as prefixes to the chassis numbers. This practice changed shortly after the introduction of the Fairway Driver because until then, each vehicle had had a separate body and chassis number. From mid-1992, the body number was discontinued. The codes should not be confused with the model names found in the brochures and workshop manuals. The codes were:

- FX4: Austin taxi with a petrol engine

- FX4D: Austin taxi with a diesel engine

- FL2: Austin Hire Car with a petrol engine

- FL2D: Austin Hire Car with a diesel engine

- FX4R: Carbodies FX4 with a 2.2-litre Land Rover petrol engine

- FL2R: Carbodies FL2 London Limousine with a 2.2-litre Land Rover petrol engine

- FL2RD: Carbodies FL2 London Limousine with a 2.2-litre Land Rover diesel engine

- FX4RD: Carbodies FX4 with a 2.2-litre Land Rover diesel engine

- FX4 RP/DS Carbodies FX4 with a 2.2-litre Land Rover petrol engine and synchromesh gearbox

- FX4 RP/D Carbodies FX4 with a 2.2-litre Land Rover petrol engine and automatic gearbox

- FX4S-PLUS D Carbodies FX4 with a 2.5 Land Rover petrol engine and automatic gearbox

- FX4S-PLUS P Carbodies FX4 with a 2.2 Land Rover petrol engine with manual or automatic gearbox

- FX4NDR Carbodies Fairway and Fairway Driver with a Nissan diesel engine and automatic gearbox

- FX4ND/S Carbodies Fairway and Fairway Driver with a Nissan diesel engine and synchromesh gearbox

pedal box. On Fairway models, this was moved to the front chassis cross-member. From 1990, the bonnet release mechanism was changed, with the bonnet release knob moved to under the dashboard on the platform side. The safety release lever remained in place.

Chassis and body numbers and commission plates

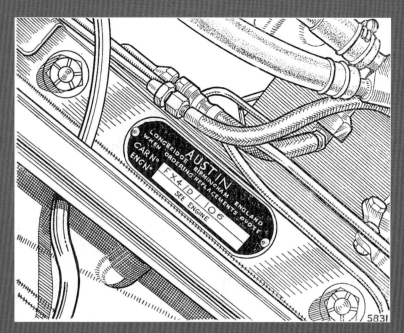

ABOVE On the first FX4 and FL2 models, the chassis number plate was fixed to the chassis leg, close to the steering box. *(London Taxi Company/Author's Collection)*

RIGHT All cabs made under the Carbodies name (FX4R onwards) carried a VIN plate fixed to the flitch plate inside the nearside front wing. This is from an FX4S-Plus and has the LTI logo. The FX4R VIN plate carried the Carbodies logo. *(Murray Jackson)*

RIGHT Fairway chassis numbers were in one of two locations, depending on age. This number is stamped on the nearside chassis leg. The prefix 'FX4NDR' identifies the cab as a Fairway with an automatic gearbox. *(Author)*

Chassis numbers

In the United Kingdom, the chassis number, now known as the VIN (Vehicle Identification Number), is the number recognised by the vehicle licensing authority, the DVLA, as the legal identity of any motor vehicle. On the Austin FX4 and FL2 this can be found in one of two locations, and is of one of two types, depending on the age of the vehicle.

Until the formation of London Taxis International, the chassis number was fixed to the offside chassis dum iron, close to the steering box on a right-hand-drive vehicle. From 1982, following the transfer of the FX4 to Carbodies, this number is found on the flitch plate under the bonnet, in front of the radiator. The chassis numbers of all cabs made under LTI were also stamped on the chassis itself, at first on the nearside chassis leg and later on the front cross-member

Commission plate

Mann & Overton fixed a commission plate to all Austin cabs, all Carbodies' FX4s and FX4Rs they sold, prior to the introduction of the FX4S. It was fitted to the partition, above the luggage platform and adjacent to the taximeter. This carried the date of the commission of the cab and the chassis number. Unless it is fixed in the manner shown, it is highly unlikely that it actually belongs to the vehicle to which it is now affixed.

BELOW On Fairways, part of the identification is also marked on the cross-member below the radiator. *(Author)*

ABOVE Every Austin and Carbodies FX4 taxi sold by Mann & Overton carried a commission plate like this one, fixed to the partition, above the luggage platform, adjacent to the taximeter bracket. This plate is not recognised by the DVLA, the UK's vehicle licensing authority as conveying the official identity of the vehicle. (*Author*)

Body numbers

Until mid-1992, each FX4 and FL2 had a separate body number. On the early FX4 and FL2 it is found on a plate fixed to the radiator mounting bracket. Subsequently, the plate was located on the edge of the scuttle, adjacent to the offside bonnet hinge. Although the VIN of early Fairway Drivers had an APAYS prefix, this was discontinued shortly afterwards. The separate body number was no longer issued and all cabs carried a single number, prefixed 'SCNDR'.

The reason for having a separate body number is historic. Carbodies, who built the FX4, had been a jobbing coachbuilder since the company's founding in 1919, putting bodies on other makers' chassis. These included MG and Railton, who did not make their own bodies. Each of their chassis had its own number, by which the licensing authorities would register the vehicle when issuing it an index mark (registration number). For the sake of its own records, Carbodies (and for that matter every other British coachbuilder) gave the body it fitted to these customers' chassis its own number, and through that number could recognise the body type and the date it was made. The FX4, and the FX3 before it, were one of many jobs Carbodies were contracted to do, and so it gave each taxi and Hire Car body its own unique number.

Note that neither the body number nor Mann & Overton's commission plate are recognised by the DVLA as the vehicle's legal identity and cannot be considered as such when transferring ownership or exporting the vehicle.

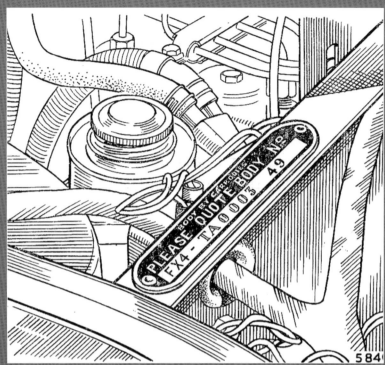

ABOVE The body plate of the first FX4s was carried on the cross-member that holds the radiator. (*London Taxi Company/Author's Collection*)

LEFT After the 1969 revision, the body number was still located on the same cross-member, but in front instead of on top. (*Author*)

LEFT On LTI cabs, until early 1992 when the system was simplified, the body number plate was mounted adjacent to the scuttle, close to the offside bonnet hinge. (*Author*)

Chapter Three

The trade's view

The FX4 in all its various guises was, for a major part of its life, the only choice the London cab trade had. Thankfully, it proved to be up to the job, and as outdated as it was in many respects, the Fairway version proved to be the best.

As practicable as it was for major cities, the cab trade in the rest of the UK, and the rest of the world, often considered it to be quite the opposite.

LEFT Cabs at London City Airport, 1992. *(Author)*

It would be too much to describe the London cab trade's relationship with the FX4 as a 'love-hate' one. Those words would be too strong, but it has been a very mixed relationship, especially for the majority of London's cab drivers. Where, say, a Ferrari owner might have a passion for his car, or a Second World War GI might have deep respect, even love, for his Jeep, it would be more accurate to say that the London cab trade gave the FX4 a grudging respect. For all the fascination the world at large may show for the London cab trade, from the inside it is not a glamorous one, even though its most familiar environment, London's West End, with its theatres and sights has a worldwide reputation for being a glamorous place.

Unlike a Ferrari, the FX4 is not a glamorous vehicle. Neither is its working environment an inherent danger, like a war zone where a Jeep would have been deployed, although parts of some of London's boroughs have an unenviable reputation. (Having said that, the design and construction of the FX4 have saved more than one driver's life in one way or another!)

So respect, even if begrudged, would sum up most London cab drivers' attitude to the FX4, and that would be as much for the cab's ability to keep going and earn all concerned a living than anything else. Properly maintained, it would start every morning, get you to work, earn you your money and get you home. With the service infrastructure that has been in place in London and other major UK cities for decades, repairs could be carried out with the minimum of downtime. It has been known for a cab with its front end smashed up in an accident, to be taken to a repair garage during the afternoon, the damaged body panels stripped off, new ones cleaned and painted and left to dry overnight, bolted on the next day and the cab be ready for work that evening. Such is the nature of both the repair facilities and the design and construction of the cab itself.

From the driver's point of view, shape and layout of the FX4, and of all type-approved London cabs as laid down by legislation based on principles of the first Conditions of Fitness for Motor Cabs, dating from 1906, has acquitted itself well. The separation of the

driver from the passengers, originally decreed in 1907 to prevent drunken or irresponsible passengers from interfering with the controls, has always given privacy to the passengers, but now provides the driver with some degree of protection from assault.

There are stories of cab drivers operating saloon cars who have been stabbed with a large blade thrust through the back of the seat, and of other drivers strangled from behind. The partition, with its glass and steel panels make such attacks either too difficult to carry out, or even contemplate. The sales success of the Fairway in Germany is down as much to the partition, and the overall construction and layout of the cab that allows its placement, as anything else. Because of the growing number of attacks on German taxi drivers, they had taken to carrying guns, which the authorities felt was inadvisable. The adoption of a vehicle that had an inherent safety feature, in the form of the partition, was a sensible move for all concerned.

The FX4 is a very practicable vehicle for the travelling public. The wide doors, with superior access on Fairway models allows people to get in and out quickly, to load wheelchairs, baby buggies, suitcases and shopping trolleys with ease, and the minimum of disruption to other traffic. Its tight turning circle allows a vehicle that is by its very nature bulky to be manoeuvred with comparative ease, enabling the cab

driver to get his passenger under way as swiftly as possible. If the Ferrari experience is about glamour (and the occasional enormous servicing bill), and if life in active combat with a Jeep is about depending on a tough and agile vehicle that will never let you down, then day-to-day life with a working FX4, or for that matter any other purpose-built taxi, is about the routine, regularity and getting on with the job. Any romance or glamour attached to the FX4 is in the mind of the outside observer!

The trade's first impressions

From the outset, the FX4 was designed so as not to look outdated, but even 15 years or so after its introduction, when it should have been replaced by something a bit more modern-looking, it was doing just that. The highly regarded Austin FX3 of 1948 was of a pre-war shape, with three doors, separate wings (and the narrow passenger space created by their inclusion), an opening windscreen and an open luggage platform. Then, in 1958, along came the FX4, with four full doors, a wider, more spacious body and a fixed windscreen. Did the London proprietors, the biggest group of customers at the time, welcome it? Not one bit!

Geoff Trotter, managing director of London's biggest fleet, the London General Cab Company, said that it was too big, too heavy and the doors opened the wrong way. Barney Davis, owner of the London East End firm, Felday Cabs was more succinct, saying: "It's just a bloody awful vehicle." Robert Overton, the chairman of dealers Mann & Overton, whose baby the FX4 was, struggled to hide his disappointment when the proprietors sounded off about the new cab. He confessed to his diary, "What a headache this is going to be!"

And it was. Not that the proprietors had much chance of evaluating it for months after its introduction, because Carbodies had such trouble making the roof that barely more than 200 were built in its first full year of production. John Birch, managing director of one of London's oldest cab firms called it a complete failure, refusing to buy any. Within three years, he had closed the cab company his family had run for a century, abandoned an ill-fated project to build a cab of his own based on a Standard Atlas van, and retired, rather than buy a vehicle he detested.

BELOW Thousands of people use a London taxi every day, appreciating the recognisability and accessibility it offers. *(Author)*

Detail faults

It was these first models that received the strongest criticism from the trade, and when in 1969 those faults were, to a greater or lesser degree corrected, the criticism was eventually turned on the dealer for selling an already outdated vehicle. Many of the early problems were a result of the build quality of the cab: its poor body pressings and its primitive rust proofing and also some inherent design faults, and what might be described as misguided economy measures. There were no weatherseals on the door windows and this allowed rainwater to pour straight down into the bottoms of the doors, causing them to rust out in just a few years. This meant that the proprietors had to spend a lot of money patching up the doors every time the cab was due for its annual overhaul.

Poorly designed rain channels under the bonnet caused water to collect under the batteries, where it rusted through the metal in around four to five years. Rainwater would then drip constantly on to the driver's right foot. Repairing this was considered an unnecessary expense by most, if not all fleet proprietors, although some owner-drivers did weld up these holes for their own comfort. Not that this was the only discomfort the driver had to tolerate.

Draught proofing was non-existent, and as the cab grew older, the body began to rattle and shake, causing gaps to appear below the doors allowing draughts to blow into both the driver's compartment and the rear. These, not surprisingly, chilled the poor passengers, who were struggling to keep warm, thanks to a totally ineffective rear heater. Although the FX3 had no passenger heater, at least it was nowhere near as draughty as the FX4!

Another penny-pinching exercise that added to driver fatigue was the omission of soundproofing. The domed bonnet of the FX4 acted like an echo chamber, and the noise of the diesel engine, already inherently loud, was augmented because of it. This level of noise also made communication between driver and passengers very difficult. It was made worse by the design of the access panel first used in the glass partition. This was a Bakelite ring set into one side of the partition glass adjacent to the driver's left ear, with a rotating glass panel

that either opened or closed the aperture. It simply wasn't big enough, and was replaced from April 1960 by a vertically sliding glass panel, mounted centrally in the partition. Even that had its drawbacks. It was mounted on a constant-balance spring and its movement was dampened by felt-covered channels. As the felt on the channels wore down with time, the dampening effect was reduced and the panel would close on its own. Replacing the channels was a difficult job that no one bothered to do, and the glass panel was usually prevented from riding up by wedging folded-up radio circuit cards or pieces of cigarette packet against it.

Transmission problems

In the FX4's early years, a significant cause of loss of earnings for the proprietors was the downtime caused by trouble with the automatic gearbox, which would break up after a relatively low mileage. The diesel engine has an inherent characteristic: a torsional vibration, which is a result of its high compression ratio. The Borg-Warner DG150M had a lock-up clutch that was engaged when the box was in top gear. If it had been coupled to a torque converter, this vibration would have been absorbed by it, but the clutch ensured that this vibration was transferred through to the transmission. The effect was to wear out the linings of the friction bands that held the transmission in gear. When the bands disintegrated, bare metal would meet bare metal and the box would give out a squeal like a banshee. All that Mann & Overton

ABOVE Herewith, evidence that early FX4s were less dependable than the later versions. This advert from *The Steering Wheel* of May 1964, shows cabs of less than two years old being sold off. Usually, a fleet would keep its cabs for at least five years, if not the full ten years allowed by the PCO. Although the garage, Halfin's, advertises manual cabs for sale, the automatic models would have been the ones they were most keen to dispose of. Two decades on, Halfin's was advertising to buy in older cabs than these. *(London Vintage Taxi Association Archive)*

could do, if the fault occurred within the six-month/6,000-mile warranty, was to replace the gearbox with another, which would also fail in due course. If it failed outside the warranty, it was a very expensive job for the proprietor.

The London General Cab Company, one of the biggest in the capital, tried to adapt the Land Rover manual gearbox to the engine, but that was a failure because the gearbox was of an old design with synchromesh on third and top gears only. The reason the fleet proprietors wanted an automatic gearbox was that they were tired of having to replace clutches, because cabmen would slip the clutch rather than change down through a heavy or crash gearbox. With the Land Rover box, cabmen would slip the clutch in third rather than crash down to second, which defeated the object of retro-fitting a manual gearbox. The fleets had to endure the troubles incurred with the auto box or carry on with the last of their FX3s until, in 1961, Austin finally offered the manual gearbox from the Gipsy 4x4. The DG150M gearbox was replaced in 1962 by the new, more suitable if not so robust, BW35 gearbox. Few proprietors bought automatic FX4s then, as the fuel consumption was higher, the performance sluggish, the transmission's life was not as long as it ought to be for a working vehicle, and the reputation for unreliability still clung to the model.

BELOW The Winchester, brought out to offer an alternative to the FX4, failed to live up to expectations. *(Author's Collection)*

Heavy controls

The manual gearbox, when it did arrive, was a pretty hefty unit. It was smooth in operation, which was certainly in its favour, but it came with an industrial-strength clutch that added further to driver fatigue. Care had to be taken, however, when starting or stopping the engine, as this caused the engine and gearbox to rock on the rubber mountings, sending the gear lever sideways and giving the driver a mighty whack on his knee with its spherical gear knob. The steering had no power assistance and, when properly set up, was manageable, but too many improperly trained mechanics would refit the kingpins incorrectly and make the steering so stiff that Hercules himself might have given up in dismay if he had to do just one more U-turn at the end of a day's shift! The brakes were heavy, too, as a servo was by no means a common piece of equipment at the time and thought unnecessary on a town vehicle.

Ineffective heaters

The heater was at least effective in keeping the driver warm, but its ability to clear mist off the windscreen was virtually nil. This ineffectiveness was compounded by the fact that the direction of the hot air was controlled by a flap under the dashboard that was spring-loaded, and the spring was prone to breaking, leaving the flap

open. When it did break, it was impossible to demist the windscreen by using hot air from the heater. The heater for the passengers was pretty poor too. It was located under the back seat, and fed from pipes that ran underneath the cab, exposed to cold air, so what water reached the heater was coldest on the days when it needed to be at its hottest.

Hobson's choice

So why did the trade put up with what seems on the face of it to be such a bad vehicle? First and foremost, it was the best option for the fleet proprietor, and to run a cab in London they had to use vehicles that were type-approved by the Public Carriage Office. The alternatives were the MkVII Beardmore and, from 1962, the Winchester. Both came from small, independent makers. The Beardmore was a quality product, with modern running gear borrowed, variously from Ford and Jaguar, but very old-fashioned in its styling. It had a coachbuilt body that had to be repaired by specialist craftsmen, who were hard to come by, and all other garages besides Beardmore's own employed men skilled in repairing steel bodies.

The Winchester, in virtually all respects, was a poor vehicle. Although it was of a modern design and had a glassfibre body that could not rust, its interior finish was

spartan; it had almost a homemade feel to it, in comparison with the coachbuilt quality of the Beardmore and the mass-produced finish of the FX4. Its Perkins diesel engine was inadequate for its job, the driving position was very uncomfortable and it was as noisy as, or possibly even noisier than, the FX4. At this time, expert glassfibre repairers were as hard, if not harder, to find than coachbuilders. Both cabs were serviced by small-scale operations based at, in Beardmore's case, three locations and in Winchester's case, just one.

ABOVE Already outdated in its styling, if not in its mechanical specification, when it was introduced in 1954, the Beardmore Mk7 never posed a threat to either the FX3 or the FX4. It remained in production until 1966, kept going because the proposed Mk8 never went into production. Its successor, through the Metro-Cammell-Weymann takeover of the manufacture of the Beardmore, was the Metrocab. *(London Vintage Taxi Association Archive)*

LEFT Even a cab involved in a major smash like this can be repaired, and in surprisingly quick time. *(Mal Smith Collection)*

Serviceability – a saving grace

On the other hand, the FX4 was an Austin, built in part by, and in part for, Britain's biggest motor manufacturer, BMC, and the network of spares supply via Mann & Overton had been built up since 1905. Getting an FX4 fixed in London would never be a problem. There were cab garages, large and small, all over the metropolis. It seemed that almost every row of railway arches in the inner suburbs had at least one cab garage, and there were some pretty big ones too, such as the London General at Brixton, Levy's at King's Cross, Stewart's in Fulham, and Coley Allen's in the East End.

If the Austin FX4 of the 1960s was never pleasant to drive, the upside was that your customers knew exactly what it was you were driving. That shape could not be mistaken for anything else. For all the advantages of such instant recognisability, it could be a nuisance when you had a passenger on board on a wet Saturday night but still people waved madly at you from the kerbside to get you to stop. And when you were not working, even outside London, people would wave you down, and stare at you in disbelief when you didn't stop for them.

Rejection by provincial operators

If any part of Britain's taxi trade wholeheartedly rejected the FX4, it was the cab drivers and operators who worked in smaller towns. The FX4 was totally wrong for their type of work, where, in a few minutes' drive from the town centre you could be in open country and long trips were a regular occurrence. On country roads in a saloon car taxi, you could be travelling at a fair speed and in comfort. In an FX4, especially an early one, you would struggle to maintain 30mph, your passengers would soon begin to feel decidedly uncomfortable, and communication with them would be all but impossible.

Even in London's slow-moving traffic, the FX4's overall performance was pretty pedantic. The diesel engine was almost agricultural in its throttle response, the automatic gearbox sapped a lot of power, and the low back axle ratio did nothing to help. Even the petrol version could only be described as a rather sedate carriage, but no proprietors, and only a handful of owner-drivers, who may have had private work, wanted a petrol cab. With a fuel consumption of 18mpg, as compared with the 25–30mpg of the diesel, a petrol engine was out of the question. Diesel engines had only been introduced to the trade in 1952, when John Birch fitted a Standard diesel adapted from the Ferguson tractor unit into an FX3. Until then, the trade was losing money because the FX3 was so thirsty.

Austin soon developed its own diesel and this was taken up almost universally. For his efforts, Birch was hailed as 'the saviour of the cab trade', an accolade he dismissed with some embarrassment. Taxi fares in London are set by Transport for London (originally the Home Office) and provincial taxi fares are set by local authorities, but private hire companies across the UK are free to set their own rates. Therefore, the provincial private hire trade, which could set its own fares could thus absorb the higher fuel costs, and those who wanted a vehicle with slightly better performance would buy petrol FL2s. So did the funeral trade, which preferred the quietness of the petrol engine to the commercial rattle of a diesel, and for whom fuel costs represented a much smaller proportion of their overheads.

The diesel engine's other virtue was its robustness and longevity. It had been offered in the FX3 for the previous four years and, despite a few initial troubles with cracks in the block and some embarrassing episodes where the odd engine went into reverse when the injector pump

BELOW June 1951: John Birch (on the right) celebrates the launch of London's first taxi with a diesel engine. *(Peter Birch)*

malfunctioned, it had become a power unit on which the trade could depend. It would run for over 100,000 miles before it needed overhauling and, in later years, even more, as oil technology had improved dramatically.

But there was no perceived need for high speed in a London taxi anyway. The cab came out a full year before the M1 motorway opened, and more than six years before the M4 extended beyond Heathrow Airport. London's traffic rarely moved above an average of 11mph. What was needed was a vehicle that the public could get in and out of easily, could load their luggage into and get out of quickly too. The FX4, like all its predecessors, provided all that. In fact, because of its comparatively low floor, it was a bit easier to get into than earlier models. This, and its turning circle, a mandatory requirement, meant that whatever other shortcomings the cab had, it still fulfilled what the Public Carriage Office required of it. It was the only cab on the market that the fleet proprietors, big or small, would entertain, which kept Mann & Overton happy (and eased Robert Overton's early headaches).

After a very short while the cab was recognised by the travelling public, and they jumped in it more and more as Carbodies finally sorted out the production difficulties. Once the major problems of transmission failure and, to some degree build quality and rust proofing had been tackled, the proprietors were beginning to be satisfied too, as the FX4 had become a reliable and serviceable vehicle. They must have begun wondering what Mann & Overton had in store for them for the 1970s.

No new model
In the previous decades, new cabs had come along at regular intervals. Mann & Overton introduced the Unic in 1906 and, although having to deal in a revised version of the same cab through the 1920s, followed it with Austin 12/4 in 1930, which lasted until the outbreak of the Second World War in 1939. The FX3 came out in 1948 and its production stopped in 1958. Beardmore had produced no fewer than six successive models between 1919 and 1939 so, as the 1960s drew towards their end, the London cab trade expected a new, more modern Austin cab.

Mann & Overton addressed the idea too, but when they received a quote for £350,000 from Carbodies for a new body built on, one presumes the old chassis, they thought this was too much money. Austin, or rather BMC, was not, it seems, approached to build a new body. They had never built one for any Austin taxi and quite likely did not have the capacity for such a small-production-run vehicle and, in any case, the arrangement with Carbodies had served them well for almost two decades. After consulting luxury sports car makers Gordon-Keeble and Jensen about a glassfibre body, Mann & Overton opted to revamp the original cab.

The proprietors were, to some degree, satisfied with this upgraded model, especially as Carbodies had made some attempts to improve the build quality in the intervening years. The changes included soundproofing under the bonnet and on the luggage platform floor, a new partition that slid open horizontally and thus stayed open, and a really effective passenger compartment heater, probably the best feature on the cab, made life more comfortable for the poor punter in winter.

The lights were changed too. They were generally disliked by most other road users, and the driver of an FX4 had to endure abuse from those who didn't, or didn't want to see, the limpet indicators on the roof. This behaviour began to occur more frequently in the late 1960s. Flashing indicators had been allowed by law since 1954, and were universally fitted to new cars from then on, but were mounted low on the body or, later, built into fins on the rear. The FX3 and the later MkVII Beardmore had limpet indicators too, and they were fitted as replacements for trafficators on older private cars, so why the poor cabman had to suffer such abuse can only be guessed. One possible answer is that the cab driver has always been a favourite target for any aggrieved road user, and not wanting to see an indicator that was actually flashing could be an excuse for such a reaction. From 1968 the roof-mounted indicators were replaced by the rear light cluster from the new MkII BMC 1100/1300, along with a small orange indicator and a repeater on the front wings. Many older-type FX4s were retrofitted with low-level indicators too.

The installation of a bigger, 2.5-litre diesel engine in 1971 helped the cab to keep up with faster traffic, made airport runs down the M4

less of a slog, and driving in general a bit less arduous, even though the brakes were still the same as they were in 1958. But with a new FX4 costing the same as a Ford Zodiac, but with much poorer performance and none of the comfort, the trade began to put pressure on Mann & Overton for a new cab. Despite the new engine and soundproofing that enabled the cabman to hear at least half of what his passenger was saying (maybe this accounts for why the London cab driver has a reputation for verbosity – he can't hear the passenger, so to be sociable he talks for both!), the rattles, squeaks and leaks were still there and it was, by now, an ageing vehicle. By the early 1970s, the only other cab on the market, the hapless Winchester, had gone to the wall and, now, the FX4 was truly Hobson's choice.

Rising prices

During the 1970s, the number of cab drivers in London began to grow. Besides this, cab fleet proprietors began to change the way they charged the driver for the hire of the cab. Originally, a cabman would operate either a day or a night shift paying a rate per mile or a percentage of the meter, changing over at around 6pm. Then, one by one, the proprietors began to charge a flat weekly rate for the hire of the cab, and cabmen decided that they would prefer to have the cab to themselves, and maximise their working hours. This reduced the ratio of drivers per cab and the demand for cabs grew.

Some of the newer drivers, having seen new, modern cars with the kind of luxury not known in their parents' time, were at the very least disappointed by the crudeness of the FX4, and its high price. A 1975 'P' registration FX4 cost, on hire purchase (HP), with interest, close on £3,650. That, as one very disgruntled cab driver put it, 'A pound a day for ten years, and for what? A pile of rubbish!'

More comfort

Despite the fact that during the 1970s cars were now offered with extras like sunroofs and vinyl roofs, these things had not been offered on the FX4. They would have been shunned by fleet proprietors as unnecessary; not one of them would earn any extra money, and the provincial operators, especially in Scotland, railed against anything that put up the price but didn't keep the running costs down, nor made cleaning them out after the weekend easier. "It's only a cab," they would say to Bill Lucas, "not a bloody limousine!"

However, the owner-driver in London, spending longer and longer hours in the driving seat, and using his cab as a family car, wanted these extras, and was willing to pay for them, especially when the cost was written into the monthly payments. The sunroof helped keep the temperature in the front down on sunny days, the vinyl on the roof was easier to clean than paint, and the different colour added a bit of individuality. While these changes didn't actually raise sales, they helped support them during the financial troubles the country was once again facing. This time it was not the three-day week, but the causes of the 'Winter of Discontent' of 1979 and its aftermath.

Brake servo fiasco

One change forced through by Mann & Overton was the installation of a servo that acted on the front brakes alone. This was condemned out of hand as bad engineering by many motor engineers inside and outside the cab trade. In practice, it made the FX4 trickier to drive, not easier. It caused the brakes to grab at slow speed, which is most often when they are used on a cab, and wore out brake linings far quicker than before. One London proprietor claimed that they were seeing an increase in brake drum wear of 70 per cent. Despite an inquiry being set up by the British Safety Council, Mann & Overton refused to budge on the issue, and told cabmen they had to learn to drive the new models differently. In an interview with Dave Barnes, the editor of *Taxi*, Mann & Overton's technical director, Mike Ray, said that a lot of the problems could be traced to the wrong brake linings, with softer ones wearing out too quickly. Other causes of wear, in older drums,

could be traced to the curvature of the new linings not matching the slightly wider diameter of the older, more worn drums. The problem was not resolved until a four-wheel servo system was introduced in 1982.

Better opportunities for women cab drivers

Up until the early 1980s, the number of women who had passed The Knowledge of London, the severe topographical and character test every London cab driver has had to undergo for over a century, could almost be counted on the fingers of one hand. Those who did succeed found that trying to cope with the FX4's heavy clutch and steering was beyond them. Now, there would be changes that would enable women to do the job without such a physical struggle. They began when Carbodies was told that the old Austin engine would no longer be available and a new engine had to be found. At this time the FX4 was the only vehicle made in the Carbodies factory.

Grant Lockhart tried other projects, but none of them was successful, so to make the factory

BELOW Legendary cab trade cartoonist Jery Craig sums up the performance of the Austin FX4's front brake-only servo. *(Jery Craig/* Taxi *Newspaper Archive)*

SORRY SIR! WE WOULD ASK OUR TRAVELLING PUBLIC TO HAVE PATIENCE WHILE THE MAKERS SORT OUT THE BRAKE PROBLEMS!!

WALLOP

SCREECH

BANG

viable, production of the FX4 had to increase and this meant tackling more provincial and overseas markets. Lockhart chose, although not, as he admitted, through 'free choice', the Land Rover diesel and, to go with it, a five-speed manual gearbox from the Rover SD1, with its light diaphragm clutch. It was also much quieter than the Austin diesel. Fitted too were full servo brakes and power steering, all of which Lockhart hoped would make the cab a more attractive proposition for the hoped-for new markets.

The arrival of the FX4R coincided more or less with an initiative by the then leader of the Greater London Council, Ken Livingstone, to open the London cab trade to women and ethnic minorities. The cab trade took umbrage at the inclusion of the term 'ethnic minorities', because The Knowledge had never been an examination that discriminated against applicants because of race or colour. Indeed, it had been a means for many Jewish refugees to escape from poverty and gain respect, and a growing number of Afro-Caribbean drivers already held London cab licences. Nevertheless, the lighter controls of the new model would make driving a London cab feasible for female drivers and their numbers have grown steadily from that time onwards.

However, the FX4R was a disaster, with the

Land Rover engine proving to be unsuitable and unreliable. Many new cabmen bought the FX4R, expecting something better than the ageing Austins they had started work with, but although the power steering and servo brakes were appreciated, most buyers were disappointed. The only section of the London cab trade who actually found any real benefit in the FX4R were those who worked at Heathrow Airport. The fleet proprietors who supplied cabs to the airport drivers who rented were, for one reason alone, happier to see the FX4R. The London and Middlesex end of the M4 motorway was built during the 1960s. The increased speed of the 2.5-litre FX4 had enabled airport drivers to do a job to 'the flyers' at somewhere around 70mph, which was flat out. As they approached the motorway slip road, it was not unknown for a connecting rod to detach itself and go through the cylinder block. The FX4R's Land Rover engine revved a good 1,000rpm higher than the Austin and the manual version had overdrive, so that model could travel at speeds of up to 100mph with no danger of the engine giving out. The downside of the cab was that it was too high-geared for town work and could not go up hills like Highgate Hill without difficulty, if at all, when loaded. Buyers of manual gearbox models were also to fall foul of the clutch and gearbox problems, when the clutch actuating arm collapsed. The plastic clutch hydraulic pipe came off when softened by the heat of the nearby exhaust, or the spigot bearing collapsed, destroying the gearbox.

The FX4R proved to be the worst vehicle to sell to new provincial markets. Despite its improved brakes and steering, its inherent unreliability made it almost universally unpopular. Compounding the dissatisfaction felt by the new customers was a poor, and in some places almost non-existent, spares and service network, a vital ingredient for any commercially operated vehicle. What made it even worse was that provincial cabmen had, for decades, bought saloon cars, either new or a couple of years old and run them for about four years, then traded them in for newer models. Carbodies maintained that an FX4R – indeed any London-type cab –was a long-term investment, as it had a working life of ten years and its resale value between, say, one and seven years was

BELOW The London Cab Company offered the free use of their brake test equipment to Westminster Insurance policyholders. Their engineering director, Roger Ward, pictured here in the white coat, was a harsh critic of the front-only brake servo and of the FX4R.
(London Vintage Taxi Association Archive)

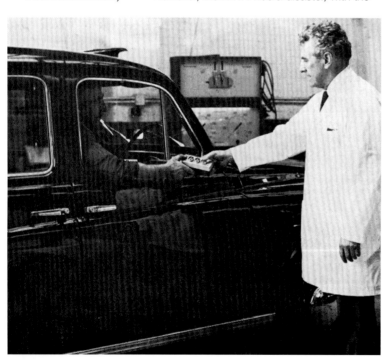

higher than a saloon car of equivalent age. The purchase price of a two-year-old Ford Cortina was noticeably less than a new FX4R, and the sums, on paper at least, made running an FX4R or two Cortinas similar, but the unreliability of the FX4R made the saloon car taxi a much better bet for the provincial operator. Only those operators in cities where the licensing authority demanded London-type cabs had to suffer the FX4R, or keep their old Austins going.

Chassis cracking

An unexpected occurrence in cabs built around 1980 was chassis cracking. The PCO suspended the licences of all cabs where they found this happening. The cracks were appearing on the lower part of the front of the chassis, behind where the front suspension was bolted. Eventually, the source of the trouble was traced to faulty manufacturing techniques. A solution was found to weld the cracked chassis, but the PCO only allowed this on cabs of four years old or less. Andrew Overton, the managing director of Mann & Overton, made an offer to the owners of any affected cabs over four years old to replace the cabs with a sound model of the same age. This whole episode sent the trade's rumourmongers and conspiracy theorists into overdrive. It was all a plot by M&O and the PCO, they said, to get users to part with their reliable Austins and buy the 'useless' Rovers. A study of the events, as shown here, proves the scaremongers to be wrong.

Another new engine

Land Rover was developing a bigger, more powerful diesel engine and it was earmarked for the FX4R, but it was introduced in Land Rovers in 1983, too late for it to go into the first Rover-engined cabs. It was finally fitted in 1985, in the FX4S. The driver had a bit more power to play with and, thanks to some bolt-on draught excluders on the door sills, a bit less of a draughty working environment, even though it was a little noisier than the FX4R.

The technology of rust-proofing had been developed, slowly, over the years and the finish of the cab was a bit better than it had been in the 1970s, and a whole lot better than in the early 1960s. Disappointing was some faulty camshaft drive belts that broke and wrecked the

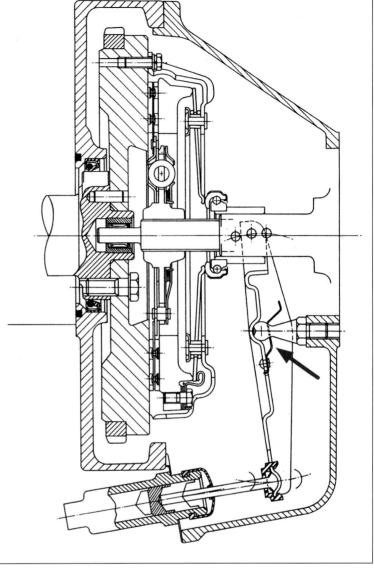

engine but, thankfully, this was a short-term problem, caused by faulty components. Another problem was the choice of engine mountings, which were not specially designed ones but the most suitable from the maker's range, and they proved not to be up to the job, causing vibration at tick-over and making the cab uncomfortable for both driver and passengers. Replacement mountings from outside manufacturers cured the problem in time. More serious was the Micronova starting system, which would flat a battery in minutes if it malfunctioned, leaving the cab driver flummoxed, furious and foul-mouthing Mann & Overton. But M&O was not to blame for this, even though irate owners let their feelings be known quite plainly to its

ABOVE The diaphragm clutch fitted to the FX4R. The troublesome stamped steel clutch actuating arm, and the ball-headed mounting post (arrowed) that eventually wore its way through it, can be seen on the lower right of the drawing. *(London Taxi Company/ London Vintage Taxi Association Archive)*

salesmen. The dealership had been sold by the owners to Manganese Bronze Holdings, who also owned Carbodies. Now everything was under one roof and decisions, good or bad, were made on their value to the vehicle alone.

The Metrocab

The trade was livened up in early 1987 by the arrival of Metrocab, made by Metro-Cammell-Weymann. This, in the words of Jamie Borwick, chairman of Carbodies owner, Manganese Bronze Holdings Plc, 'terrified' the company. Here was a completely modern vehicle with seats for five passengers, plenty of headroom for the driver, no draughts or leaks and, thanks to a glassfibre body, no rust. Crucially, it was fully wheelchair-accessible, a feature that had been incorporated in the two CR6 prototypes.

Now there was some real competition, and for a short period in the summer of 1988, the Metrocabs outsold the FX4S.

A welcome for the FX4S-Plus

This was a major challenge to Carbodies but they were already on the case, with a revised model, the FX4S-Plus. This also seated five passengers and, in a new, smart grey interior and a revamped driver's compartment, had a moulded grey plastic dashboard and a more comfortable seat. At last the cab driver was treated with some respect, even if it was through a revamp of a superannuated vehicle of which the trade had already had enough. It was launched at the Taxi Driver of the Year Show, held every Autumn in Battersea Park. Andrew Overton was there and recalls being overwhelmed by the response the cab received, everyone praising its comfort and new style.

The trade still did not invest a lot in the 'Plus': sales were hovering around the same 2,000-plus as they were a decade previously, despite there being a 20 per cent increase in the number of cabs licensed in London in the mid-1980s. Much of this was accounted for by sales of over 900 Metrocabs in 1988, the first full year of production of the FX4S-Plus. Also, a relaxation by the PCO of their ten-year age limit had allowed proprietors to hang on to their 1970s Austins, which although ageing, were reliable and, for the most part, paid for.

Delight with the Fairway

If there was some degree of satisfaction with the S-Plus, then the trade as a whole was delighted with the Fairway because, quite simply, it was by far the best version of the FX4 ever built, with easily the best engine ever installed in a London taxi of any make. The interior finish was the same as the S-Plus, with the addition of wheelchair accessibility and, on higher-spec models, a sliding sunroof in place of the front hinged one that had been used since the late 1970s. However, most praise was reserved for the 2.7-litre Nissan diesel and the four-speed automatic gearbox that was ordered with almost all Fairways sold in London. The engine was smooth, quiet and powerful, and in time proved itself to be virtually bombproof.

Sales broke all records for its introductory year, 1989, and the year following. If it hadn't been for yet another slump in the UK economy, 1991 would have been as good, if not better.

Fleet proprietors and owner-drivers alike, who had avoided buying either the FX4R or FX4S, were trading in their old Austins for new Fairways. Even better was the Fairway Driver of 1992, with its disc brakes and new front suspension. This was not without one terrifying fault: steering shimmy. At speeds of over 35mph, if the front wheels hit a bump the steering wheel would vibrate violently, all but throwing the driver's hands off the steering wheel. The only way to stop it was to bring the cab down to around 20mph and accelerate gradually away. Initially, LTI denied that the fault occurred, which angered everyone who experienced it, and they felt that even though Mann & Overton were now part of the same company as the makers, nothing had changed so far as the treatment of the customers was concerned. Eventually, the problem was cured by the fitting of a steering damper to new cabs and retrofitting on existing ones.

The Fairway in provincial markets

LTI targeted the provincial markets aggressively with the Fairway. The main weapon was wheelchair accessibility, which had government backing, as the Department of Transport had

ABOVE Greater Manchester has several licensing areas within its boundaries. This picture shows cabs ranking at Manchester Victoria station in the early 1990s. 'On point' is an FX4R and behind it are an FX4S and an Austin FX4, followed by a Metrocab. *(Author)*

ABOVE **Blackpool is one UK town that has operated a so-called 'mixed fleet' of London-type cabs and saloon cars for many years. The licensing authority allowed the fitting of a seat beside the driver in FX4s which, traditionally, were known as 'bombers'.** *(Ross Campbell)*

sponsored legislation that would make this mandatory on all purpose-built taxis. Now, LTI's sales people homed in on local authorities, which were, and still are, responsible for all taxi and private hire legislation. These authorities have the power to specify what types of vehicle they permit for use as taxis, and the great majority had allowed private cars to be used as taxis for decades. Only the big metropolitan authorities like Birmingham, Manchester, Glasgow and Edinburgh insisted on London-type cabs.

Now the provincial cab trade was, once more, having to face the FX4 (and for that matter the Metrocab) being placed before them. They remembered what had happened

with the FX4R and many fought hard against what they saw as an unnecessary and overly expensive intrusion into the sound and proven working practices they had continued for years. One of their arguments was that most people who are confined to wheelchairs are not in regular work and do not earn sufficient money to be able to afford taxis for frequent transport. Neither, if they had become disabled, would they deliberately move into the country and away from cities and the wider range of support services that were available to them. London had, and still has, its Taxicard scheme, providing subsidised travel for disabled people, whether wheelchair-bound or not. Such a scheme was rare or non-existent outside the capital, so why, the provincial trade argued, should they buy a vehicle that was significantly more expensive, and less reliable than their choice of private car, when there was little or no demand for its specialist facility?

The matter was eventually settled, in different ways in different places, to varied degrees of acceptance. Some authorities allowed a 'mixed fleet' of private cars and purpose-built cabs. Others insisted on London-type cabs only. Others found a compromise, to the satisfaction of the entire trade or otherwise. Provincial licensing authorities have the power to limit the number of hackney carriage (i.e. taxi) plates they issue. It is in the hackney carriage trade's interest both in regard to their own prosperity and the safe maintenance of their vehicles, to keep the number of hackney plates to such a level that meets demand, but does not swamp the market.

Most licensing authorities respect this balance, but some chose to issue new plates to purpose-built taxis, thus increasing the fleet and meeting a (rightly or wrongly) perceived level of need for wheelchair-accessible vehicles. Feelings about the Fairway were more widely varied outside the capital than inside, with some drivers and proprietors praising their robustness and the passengers' love of them, while others declared the complete opposite. The differences in opinion of disabled passengers was even more marked.

LEFT **The Mayor of London, Boris Johnson, brought about the end of the FX4 with new clean-air legislation.** *(James O. Jenkins/GLA)*

As many of them living in the provinces said that they found the Fairway too difficult to get in and out of, as did those in London who found them far easier to access than the private cars used by minicab companies.

By the end of the 1990s, the FX4 was eventually replaced. LTI's next model, the TX1, proved a runaway success, having all the mechanical components of the Fairway but with a tight, modern, leak-proof and rattle-free bodyshell, and a lot of Fairways were traded in. Those who hung on to their older Fairways, or had traded up from an earlier one to a later one, were glad to have kept them after the next model, the TXII came out. Its Ford DuraTorq engine and drivetrain were troublesome, but around 2005 there was pressure for Fairway owners to trade up to them. The Greater London Authority (GLA) is ever mindful of air quality in the capital, and rightly so, but in attempting to deal with traffic pollution, they homed in on the cab trade, insisting that all cabs from 2007 should comply with the Euro 3 directive on exhaust emissions. This meant that all Fairways and older cabs, as well as some of the early TX1s which were fitted with the same Nissan engine, would have to come off the road, unless they could be fitted with equipment that cleaned up the exhaust gasses.

Suitable equipment was developed, which resulted in a choice of either an exhaust recirculating system or a turbocharger. This would allow the cabs to keep working for a few more years, but at a price of close on £2,000 per cab. The option was to buy a TXII, as second-hand TX1s were like gold dust, with dealers only selling traded-in models to fleet proprietors. Faced with this situation, a great many Fairway owners, both fleet proprietors and owner-drivers, opted to spend the money to convert their trusted Fairways rather than buy a suspect TXII. Mileages in excess of 450,000 are not uncommon with some older Fairways still working in London, some of which could be over 20 years old.

The GLA had the last word. In 2010, it was announced that, because of the UK government's Air Quality Strategy, all cabs over 15 years old would no longer be licensed after 1 January 2012. The majority of Fairways on London's streets are already older, and by 2013 the very last, built in 1997, will have to be withdrawn from service.

Black cabs and bales of hay

A taxi driver has to keep a bale of hay in his cab, even though he doesn't have a horse. That's right, isn't it? Everyone knows that! Well, no. Tired of always hearing this old chestnut, Jack Everitt, a former Senior Vehicle Examiner at the Public Carriage Office, decided to scour through the many rules and regulations that control the London cab trade. He could not find any such rule anywhere that related to motor cabs. There was, and still is, a requirement for horse cab drivers to keep 'bait', i.e. hard food such as oats and chaff for his horse, but that applies strictly to horse cabmen. So now you know.

Another myth is that by law all cabs in London must be black. That's right, too, isn't it? If it is, then plenty of cab proprietors are breaking the law every day – just look through the pages of this book and see how many are not black! Some are blue, some are maroon, while others have a colourful advertising livery. So why are they called, 'black cabs'?

Before the Second World War, cabs were painted in many different colours, and a fleet would generally keep all its cabs painted the same colour, be it blue, maroon, green or brown, simply so that they only had to keep one colour of paint in the stores. (Plus of course black, for the wings!) In fact, cabs would be ordered from the dealers in a choice of colours. Austins came in red or blue, Beardmores, in the 1930s at least, in blue, maroon or green, and Morris-Commercial cabs were at first tan and later blue. These all had coachbuilt bodies and the special coach paint applied to them would flex with the body.

When the Nuffield Oxford came out in 1947, followed by the Austin FX3 in 1948, they both had pressed steel bodies, and were painted in a standard black cellulose, which happened to be the colour that dried quickest. (In fact, that's why Henry Ford said you could have a Model T in any colour so long as it was black – it dried the quickest and so was cheapest to use!) Cabs could be had in other colours, but at extra cost, and as a blue cab didn't earn any more money than a black one, hardly anyone ordered a different colour cab. When the Beardmore Mk7 and the FX4 came out, they too came in a standard colour. Beardmores could be had with an overspray of maroon or blue, but few people took up the option. Only the Winchester of 1962 bucked the trend, with its two-tone grey paint, but the later models were all painted black.

So, almost all London taxis were black. When the minicabs arrived, and the dust settled after the initial heated conflict, many men saw minicabbing as a way into becoming a taxi driver, so long as they could meet the strict requirement of having no criminal record, and a clean bill of health. The Public Carriage Office never used the term 'taxi' in official correspondence, preferring the term 'cab'. Laws were passed preventing minicab operators from using the word 'cab' in any advertising or promotion, but nevertheless the minicab trade usurped the word 'cab' for their own use. To distinguish themselves from the licensed trade, minicab people always talked of their vehicles as 'cabs' and the original licensed cabs – taxis - as 'black cabs'. Thus the term was brought into common use. Perversely, the London Taxi Company, the firm that was once Carbodies and then London Taxis International, say that silver is almost as popular a colour now for new cabs as black!

Chapter Four

The mechanic's view

The reason why the FX4 was so right for its job was that it was a simple, robust vehicle that could be easily fixed. These qualities also make it a good vehicle for the enthusiast to own. The diesel engines fitted to almost all models are nothing to be afraid of, once the difference in the way the fuel system operates is understood. Almost all the mechanical and electrical components are sourced from BMC or British Leyland vehicles, or British or British-based component suppliers such as Lucas, Lockheed and GKN, and are easy to source.

LEFT A mixture of Austin cabs – FX4s, FX3s and a single, retired 12/4 FL from the late 1930s occupy one of the workshops of the London General Cab Company's workshops, c. 1960. *(Mal Smith Collection)*

115

THE MECHANIC'S VIEW

Safety first

Motor vehicles are as dangerous, if not
more so, when they are being repaired
than when they are out on the road. Because
as are not moving, it is easy to think that danger
is not present, but serious or even fatal injuries
can occur if proper equipment is not used and
the right clothing worn.

Personal safety

- Wear clean mechanic's overalls and strong
  shoes or boots, preferably with steel
  toecaps. If you have long hair, it can get
  caught in things like a moving fan belt,
  so tuck it out of the way under a hat or a
  hairnet. Remove all jewellery, including rings,
  as metal conducts electricity and heat, and
  can give you a shock or a burn.
- Wear latex gloves and use a barrier cream
  on your hands. Used diesel oil is the filthiest
  substance you'll ever come across in motor
  vehicle repair and very difficult, if not almost
  impossible, to get off your fingers. It is also
  potentially carcinogenic.
- Lift heavy objects by keeping your back
  straight and using your leg muscles. Never
  try to lift a large, heavy object like an engine,
  gearbox or back axle, or anything that
  weighs more than about 120lb (55kg) on
  your own, if it is large, awkward, has sharp
  edges, or is in a confined space. Don't be a
  hero and don't be impatient: always play safe
  and either use lifting equipment or get help.

- When working with mains-operated power
  tools, always be careful not to get the lead
  tangled. Use a circuit breaker and ensure the
  tools are properly earthed.
- When sanding or grinding down rust or old
  paint, always wear goggles and respiratory
  protection. Old paints can contain lead
  compounds, which are potentially injurious.
  Dust can cause serious health problems and
  sparks from a grinding wheel can burn plastic
  spectacle lenses.
- Do not spray paint or other fluids without wearing
  proper protective clothing and respiratory
  protection. Also wear respiratory protection when
  cleaning out clutch housings and brake drums to
  protect yourself from the dust.

Potential hazards

- Never run an internal combustion engine in
  a confined space. Carbon monoxide fumes
  are poisonous and can cause permanent
  brain damage and death. Exhaust fumes from
  diesel engines contain particulates and other
  substances that are hazardous to human health.
- If you do not have access to a hoist or a pit,
  make sure you have good axle stands, a trolley
  jack and service ramps and learn how to use
  them all properly. If one-half of the vehicle is
  jacked up, ensure the wheels that are on the
  ground are properly chocked. When you jack
  up a vehicle always, if you have to remove any
  road wheels, loosen the wheel nuts before
  jacking the vehicle, and when replacing them,
  tighten them fully after the vehicle has been
  lowered. Always make sure you place the jack
  in a good position, on firm ground and under a
  sound part of the chassis so that it will lift the
  vehicle high enough for you to place an axle
  stand underneath the vehicle without the jack
  being raised to its maximum. Always place axle
  stands so that they do not get in the way of the
  part of the vehicle you will be working on. Never
  crawl under a vehicle that is only supported on
  a jack or, worse, bricks or blocks of wood.
- Ensure that a motor vehicle is not in gear when
  you start the engine. An inhibitor switch should
  prevent a vehicle with an automatic transmission
  from starting while it is in gear, but these do
  malfunction and it is not unknown for them to
  be bypassed, so select 'park' before attempting
  to start the engine. Also, worn or badly adjusted

selector rods on an automatic Austin FX4 can give a false reading on the indicator, so make sure the lever is moved so that the needle is as far as it can go to the right.

■ Never remove the radiator or expansion tank cap while the engine is hot. Let everything cool down before you start work.

■ Always disconnect the battery when working on a motor vehicle. If you work on a vehicle with the battery connected, you may touch a supply lead to the earth, causing a short circuit and risking a fire. Disconnect the earth lead first. If you disconnect the power lead first, your spanner may slip and complete a circuit between the terminal and the vehicle.

■ Be careful with jump leads. Always connect one lead at a time, connecting both ends of the red leads to the corresponding positive terminals before connecting both ends of the black leads to the correct negative terminals. Never jump-start a vehicle that has positive earth from a vehicle that has negative earth, or vice versa.

■ On a petrol engine, the high-tension side of the coil can give you a hefty shock, which, apart from being unpleasant, can be dangerous for someone with heart problems.

■ The sulphuric acid in a car battery can cause burns and skin irritation, as well as burn clothing. Take care when topping up the battery and never allow a naked flame near the battery – the cells give off highly inflammable hydrogen gas.

■ Petrol is highly inflammable and petrol vapour is explosive, so never smoke or permit naked

flames near the fuel system. Never let fuel spill on to a hot engine. Never work on the cab's fuel system with it placed over an inspection pit – fuel vapour is not only toxic, it is heavier than air and will sink into the pit. Diesel fuel is especially toxic and its fumes can cause headaches and nausea.

Diesel injection pumps operate at very high pressure. The spray from an injector can actually penetrate the skin and possibly be fatal, so be very careful when working on fuel injectors and fuel pipes. Always leave the servicing of injectors to specialist companies who have the right equipment to do the job.

■ Never siphon fuel, engine oil, antifreeze or brake fluid out of a container by sucking on a pipe. If you do, and either get some in your mouth or swallow it, seek medical assistance immediately.

■ Used engine oil is dangerous: prolonged contact with it can cause skin cancer, so keep your hands clean, launder your overalls regularly and never keep them on for longer than necessary. Use latex gloves and a barrier cream on your hands. These gloves can be bought cheaply in bulk, and they will keep your hands a lot cleaner than commercial hand cleaners will!

■ Asbestos dust can cause cancer if inhaled or swallowed. Asbestos was once used in gaskets and brake and clutch linings. No car spares are sold these days that contain asbestos, but you are dealing with an old vehicle that may have been laid up for some time and might still have parts made with asbestos. There is also a chance that some new-old-stock parts bought, for instance, at an autojumble from an unwitting or unscrupulous trader may contain it. In any event, wear respiratory protection when cleaning out clutch housings and brake drums.

Tools and working facilities

Do not try to work on any motor vehicle without a proper workshop manual. Workshop manuals and parts catalogues can be sourced online, and members of the London Vintage Taxi Association can buy these for most models on CD-Rom from the club.

With certain exceptions, the threads on all components of an FX4 are to American SAE standards, having UNF or UNC threads, so you will need AF spanners. The exceptions are the Nissan engine and transmissions in the Fairway models, the 3-litre Perkins Phaser, and the Nissan TD25 engines that were fitted as a conversion in the FX4R and FX4S, which have metric threads. (These latter engines were mated to the original manual or automatic transmissions, which have SAE threads.) For distributors fitted to Austin and Land Rover petrol engines you will need BA spanners.

Most work can be done with the kind of tools found in the average enthusiast's toolbox. A certain number of specialist tools are listed in the workshop manuals, but the great majority of these are pullers of various types, piston ring compressors and coil spring compressors, as well as drifts and hub bearing replacement tools that are either in general use or can either be made or modified from other tools.

Notes on maintaining an FX4

Because so much of the FX4's mechanical components are derived from standard BMC cars of the 1950s, they are very simple to maintain, even if some tasks require a certain amount of expertise to ensure that they are done correctly. The FX4 needs about as much servicing as a contemporary car.

Engines

Parts for overhauling the Austin and Land Rover engines are still available, and the engines themselves are straightforward to overhaul. Very few Nissan engines have 'given up the ghost', as it were, but it should be noted that if the bores have worn, they cannot be over-bored. They need to be re-sleeved.

The fuel system

Until recently, diesel engines were not popular in Britain, although they have gained an enthusiastic following since fuel prices became truly extortionate. In the USA, Canada and New Zealand, diesel cars and light trucks are almost unknown outside the trucking industry, although light diesel vehicles are common in Australia. It is not too difficult to find repairers in Britain and Europe, but harder to find someone in the

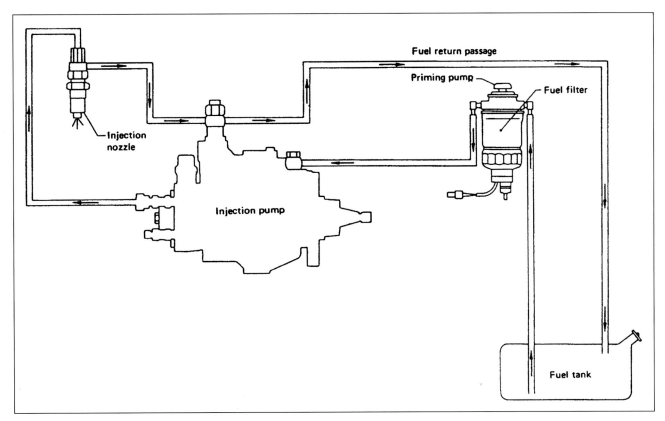

Fuel return passage

Priming pump

Fuel filter

Injection nozzle

Injection pump

Fuel tank

USA, New Zealand or Canada who knows what they are doing. Whatever their frequency, most people are mystified by them, but they are not difficult to maintain once it is understood how they work.

They work just like a four-stroke petrol engine, with the exception of how the fuel is delivered and ignited. In a petrol engine, an air/fuel mixture is drawn through the inlet manifold into the cylinders, where it is compressed and ignited by a spark plug. In a diesel engine, only air is drawn into the cylinders, and the fuel is sprayed at high pressure into the combustion chamber, where the heat generated by a compression ratio around twice as high as in a petrol engine causes the atomised fuel to ignite. In actual fact, all the engines fitted to FX4s are of the Ricardo 'Comet' indirect injection type. In this design of engine, the actual combustion chambers are cast into the piston crowns, rather than into the head. Built into the head casting are pre-combustion chambers, one for each cylinder. The injectors spray fuel into these pre-combustion chambers and the burning fuel shoots through a small pipe that leads into the cylinder bore, powering the piston.

To ensure a sufficiently fine spray of fuel is produced by the injectors, the fuel is pumped under high pressure by the injector pump. The nozzles of the injectors also need to be set correctly. Cleanliness is vital in the fuel system of a diesel engine. The injector pump is lubricated by the fuel, so any dirt in the fuel system will damage the pump, and this is an expensive piece of equipment to repair, if indeed you can find somewhere where you live to carry out the job. A fault occasionally encountered with Austin and Land Rover diesels is a sticking injector. This occurs when a small piece of dirt gets caught in the spray nozzle. Suddenly, the engine will begin to knock violently, sounding as if a big end has gone. It is simple to cure: just bring the cab to a standstill, leave the engine running and rev it hard, so as to force the dirt out of the nozzle through the sheer pressure of the injector pump. You should be sure, of course, that it actually is a sticking injector, and not a worn out bearing! The noise is different, though. The noise of a worn bearing has a metallic ring to it, whereas a sticking injector does not.

Starting a diesel engine requires everything about it to be in sound condition. The heater

ABOVE Diagrammatic of the fuel flow system. This simple chart shows the flow of fuel to the Nissan diesel engine in the Fairway series. The 2.5-litre Land Rover engine in the FX4S and S-Plus used a similar setup, while models with Austin and 2.3-litre Land Rover engines had a mechanical lift pump between the fuel tank and the fuel filter. *(London Taxi Company/ London Vintage Taxi Association Archive)*

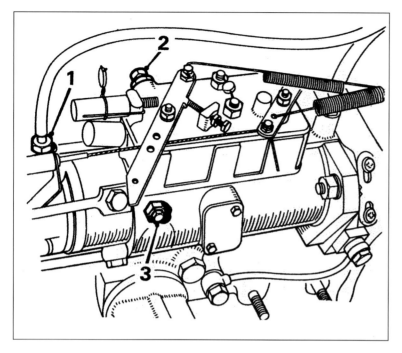

ABOVE On all models up to and including the FX4R, if the fuel system was stripped for maintenance, or the vehicle ran out of fuel, the system had to be bled to remove air. This involved unscrewing various joints and bleed valves, including these numbered here on the injector pump. *(London Taxi Company/London Vintage Taxi Association Archive)*

BELOW Diesel fuel injectors are complex and finely engineered, and it is important to have them properly serviced. This job is best left to experts and the money spent will repay itself in improved fuel consumption, performance, better starting, and cleaner exhaust. The injectors fitted to a Nissan diesel need the least amount of servicing; those fitted to Land Rover diesels need servicing most frequently. *(London Taxi Company/London Vintage Taxi Association Archive)*

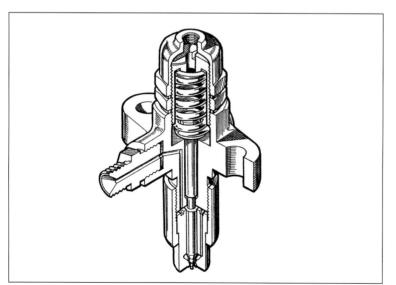

plugs, which preheat the pre-combustion chambers to aid starting from cold must all be working, the injectors must be properly serviced, the compression good, the lift pump working properly, the injector pump in good condition and, above all, the battery must be in top condition and of the right size for the job. Too small a battery will never provide enough guts to start a hefty engine with a sumpful of thick, cold oil and a 20:1 compression ratio.

Under no circumstances whatsoever, should you use a spray 'quick-start' fluid. This will cause permanent damage to the engine. If your engine doesn't start properly, fix the things mentioned above rather than take the short-term easy solution. Ensuring that the fuel system is clean is the reason why the fuel filter is changed according to the service schedule. Blockage will also cause poor running. Don't forget one thing when starting an Austin FX4: push the fuel stop knob in first! Without doing so, you will *never* start the engine!

A small filter is fitted inside the fuel tank, adjacent to where the fuel pipe is bolted, to prevent sediment from entering the fuel system. In time this can become blocked by rust and dirt or, in very cold weather the water that settles in the bottom of the fuel tank may freeze around the filter, preventing fuel from flowing. Remove this filter and clean it to prevent trouble.

The inner fabric of the venturi hose on pre-1969 FX4s can collapse, restricting the air to the engine. If this happens, replace a

BELOW The corrugated hose, the venturi hose on this particular 1970 Austin, is plastic and a far better option than the fabric one used on earlier models. *(Author)*

fabric hose with the plastic one used on all
subsequent models. Better still, replace it
before it happens.

The cooling system

Three types of radiator can be found on FX4s,
depending on the age of the cab, and these
must be in sound condition if overheating
is to be avoided. The pre-1969 type is
unpressurised. It was as a matter of course
filled with tap water in milder weather and this
caused the block and head to rust, which
would clog up the cores of the radiator. This
in turn would cause the cab to overheat and,
in an attempt to prevent overheating, some
less-than-thorough proprietors would remove
the thermostat. If a thermostat was refitted,
but the radiator not cleaned out, then the cab
would boil over when put to harder work than
usual. There is no substitute for a sound, clean
radiator. If it is sound but dirty, get it cleaned. If
it is in poor condition, get it re-cored. You will
reap the benefits in smoother running, better
fuel economy and peace of mind.

The pressurised types, large and small, that
are fitted to all models after 1969 also need to
be in sound condition and with the right type of
pressure cap fitted to the expansion tank, *not*
the radiator itself. The cap for the radiator must
be an unpressurised one. These were required
to be filled with antifreeze all year round, but by
no means did this happen, especially when the
cab got older and less money was spent by
some on maintenance. On all cooling systems,
ensure that the radiator and heater hoses are
sound, that a thermostat is fitted and, on a
pressurised system, the right type of pressure
cap is in place.

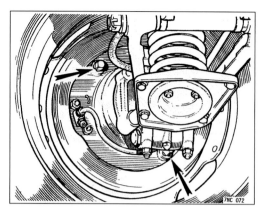

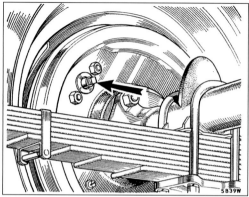

RIGHT Each of the front brake shoes on cabs up to early 1992 are adjusted by the square-headed bolts indicated. *(London Taxi Company/London Vintage Taxi Association Archive)*

FAR RIGHT The rear brake shoes are adjusted by the squared end of the wedge-type adjuster, indicated. *(London Taxi Company/Author's Collection)*

Transmissions

The manual gearboxes fitted to FX4s are, in general, robust units although the five-speed Rover box was prone to damage when the input shaft bearing collapsed. Unless you have a higher degree of skill than the average enthusiast (if there is indeed such a thing), repair of these is best left to the expert.

Maintenance and repair of automatic transmissions and power-assisted steering boxes need more specialist equipment, but all types used on the FX4 are known to the trade and can be repaired without too much trouble.

However, repairing or servicing an automatic transmission is not a cheap job, and is one that is best left to experts, who have all the necessary equipment, spare parts and the spotlessly clean working conditions necessary for the job.

Brakes

The brakes on all models up to early 1992 have to be adjusted manually by using a special brake spanner with a square aperture on a head protruding from the back plate. The front brake shoes are adjusted via a snail cam, while on the

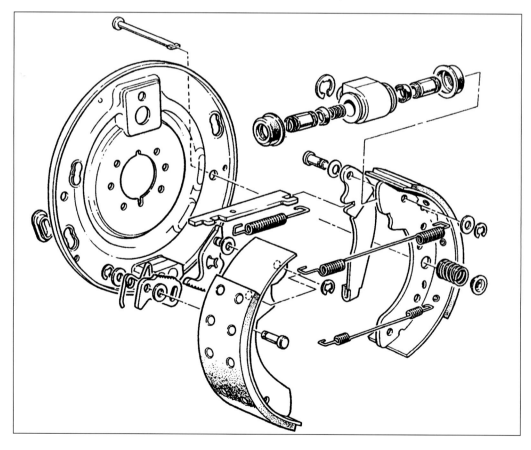

RIGHT The rear brakes fitted to the Fairway Driver and Fairway 95 are self-adjusting. *(London Taxi Company/London Vintage Taxi Association Archive)*

back brakes, a large bolt with a tapered end pushes two pistons against the upper ends of the shoes. The rear adjusters are liable to seize up through rust or a build-up of brake dust and grease. If this happens, they can be removed and soaked overnight in paraffin or WD40, but if they are too far gone, they will need to be replaced.

The brake shoes rest against steady posts, which are small pins screwed into the back plate. Each has a small white plastic cap upon which the actual brake shoe rests and allows the shoe to move more easily than if it bore on bare metal. The purpose of these posts is to ensure the brake shoes face squarely on to the drum surfaces. If the brakes have been too tightly adjusted and have overheated, the heat will have melted the caps, and caused them to be squashed by the pressure of the hold-off springs. If this has happened, the brake shoes will then not be square on to the drums and will wear unevenly The steady post caps, which are very cheap items, will have to be replaced to allow the shoes to be properly aligned.

If the handbrake appears to need adjusting on any model prior to the Fairway Driver, then the back brakes either need taking up or relining. *Never* take up wear in the handbrake by adjusting the operating rods. It is almost never known for these to have stretched. On a Fairway Driver, however, the handbrake cable will wear or stretch in time and need replacing.

Front suspension and steering

On models without power steering, a certain amount of free play is permissible in the steering box, but not too much. On models with power steering, take care when starting up on a cold day, or when you have left the cab standing for some time. The steering box is the same type as that used on a Range Rover, but is mounted upside down, so that the seal for the drag link shaft is at the bottom. In cold weather, the casing contracts and the seal is less effective than when at operating temperature. When starting from cold, allow the engine to run for a couple of minutes so that the fluid in the steering pump has warmed, and thus warmed up the oil, and the seal is more effective. The steering joints are the normal type found on most British cars and are changed in the same way.

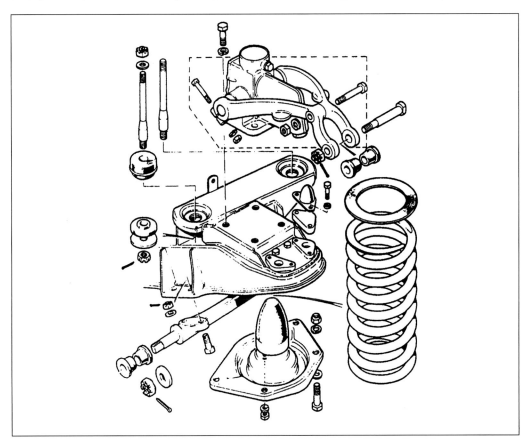

LEFT **Part of the front suspension used on all models up to 1992, showing the axle beam, spring, spring seat and shock absorber.** *(London Taxi Company/London Vintage Taxi Association Archive)*

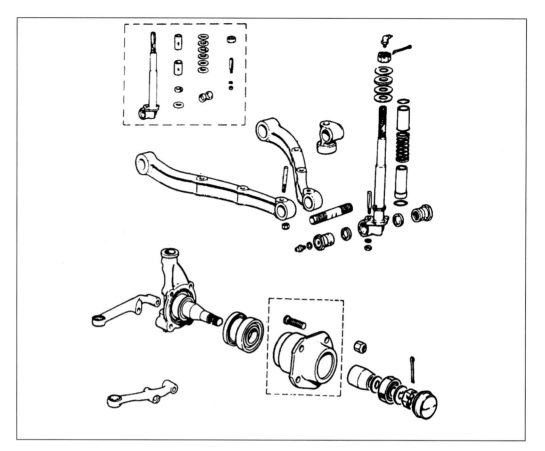

RIGHT Part of the front suspension and steering used on all models up to 1992, showing the lower wishbones, kingpins, swivel axle, fulcrum pins and hub. *(London Taxi Company/London Vintage Taxi Association Archive)*

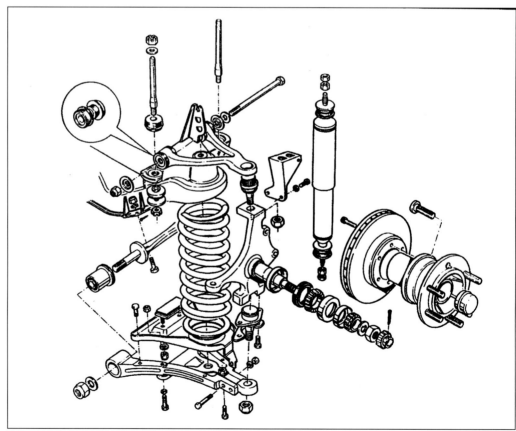

RIGHT The front suspension of the Fairway Driver, in exploded form. *(London Taxi Company/ London Vintage Taxi Association Archive)*

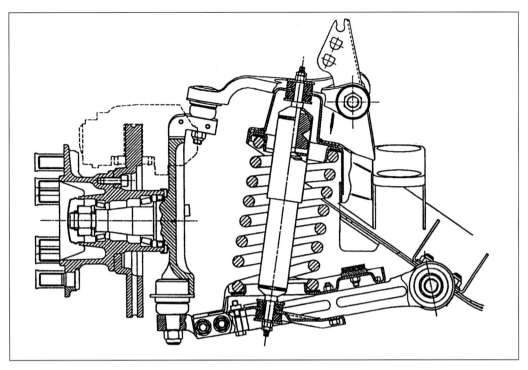

The kingpins need to be correctly assembled to ensure proper wear. Incorrect assembly can result in the steering becoming too heavy, which makes the cab very unpleasant to drive. It can also cause unnecessary wear in the lower wishbone rubbers. Special hard plastic bushes can be found, which are sold in the mistaken attempt to 'cure' a problem that was unavoidable in the first place.

The electrical system

The insulation around electrical wiring will dry and perish in time, and on an older cab it may be necessary to rewire part, or all, of the vehicle. This is a long tricky job, but there is no short cut if the wiring is beyond repair. Earth connections can become corroded, so it is always worthwhile unscrewing them and cleaning them up. A fault that can occur on early cabs is that the grommet through which the headlamp wiring passes can fall out, allowing the wire to rub against the body and eventually wear down to the bare wire. This can cause the lights on one side of the cab to short out. Replace the grommet and the damaged section of the wire.

The wiring to the nearside tail lights on Fairways is not secured in the best way it could be, and if the wheelchair ramps are removed, it is easy to catch the indicator wire with the end of the ramp. This will cause the indicators to

malfunction. The remedy is easy – just clip the wire back into its bullet connector! Some S-Plus and Fairway headlight switches were faulty, but most were replaced by sound ones, so if the headlights fail on one of these models, suspect the light switch.

The annual steam clean of any London cab prior to its overhaul can be a blessing so far as keeping chassis rust away, but it can in time affect the electrical components, particularly the fuse boxes of earlier models, up to and including the FX4S. These were located under the bonnet and moisture collected in them, gradually causing corrosion. FX4S-Plus and Fairway fuse boxes were not exempt from problems either. These are located under the dash adjacent to the driver's right leg and swing down on a hinge for access.

The windscreens of all FX4s are prone to leak, especially if the top of the seal has been broken by the installation of a vinyl roof and water can, and does, drip down on to the fuses, causing corrosion and short-circuiting. Most drivers kept the fuse box unclipped and hanging down to prevent this happening, and it is a good idea to do the same if your cab is kept in the open for any length of time.

Tips on driving your FX4

Regular use of any motor vehicle helps keep it in good condition. Brakes can seize, oil can drain down from the tops of the gears in differentials and gearboxes and cause them to go rusty. Even if you only go around the block a couple of times, do use your cab regularly.

When driving a cab with an automatic transmission, do not take it out of gear when stopped at traffic lights. Leave it in 'drive' and pull the handbrake on. Constantly taking it out of gear and re-engaging gear during normal driving can wear out the internal mechanism quickly. However, if you leave the engine running when you get out of the vehicle, always place the transmission in 'park'.

If you use your cab infrequently, you may have fuel trouble, and there are two reasons for this. One is that although diesel fuel is not as volatile as petrol, it does contain volatile ingredients which are vital for combustion. These evaporate in time, reducing the effectiveness of the fuel and making it harder, or in some cases impossible, to start. The second reason is that diesel fuel contains a small amount of water, which will separate out if the cab is left for any length of time. Bacteria and microscopic fungi can find their way into the fuel tank and live on the boundary of the two fluids, devouring the fuel, and will leave a deposit that will, at best, prevent your engine from running properly and, at worst, cause harm to it.

This problem, known as 'diesel bug', is one that boat owners are familiar with, as light craft are often left unattended for longer periods, but it is little known in commercial vehicles, as most diesel vehicles are worked regularly and the fuel is constantly being used up and replenished. However, a preserved vehicle with a diesel engine will have infrequent use, so this problem may well occur. Prevention is achieved by either using your cab regularly and keeping the tank as full as possible between uses, or if the cab is used infrequently, by draining the tank regularly or at least by not keeping a great amount of fuel in the tank. The cure for 'diesel bug' is to clean the tank and the fuel system, using a proprietary cleaning agent.

Lubrication and servicing

Below is a very much simplified version of what the handbooks say should be carried out, and is given as a guide to the prospective owner so that they can appreciate the relatively modest level of work required to maintain an FX4 of any age. If you buy an FX4 check the handbook for the full service schedule.

All models
Daily:
- Check the engine oil level and water level in the radiator and top up if necessary.

Weekly:
- Check the levels in the brake fluid reservoir and, where fitted, the power-steering reservoir and top up if necessary. An excessive drop in levels in these reservoirs indicates a leak somewhere, so examine the inside of the wheels for any signs of brake fluid leakage, and the floor below the steering box for any signs of leaks from the steering box, and attend to any problems discovered before attempting to drive the vehicle.

Austin and Land Rover diesel and petrol models
Every 3,000 miles or 3 months:
- Change engine oil and filter.
- Grease all front suspension and steering joints and propshaft universal joints. Adjust front and rear brakes.

Every 12,000 miles:
- Change fuel filter (diesel engines only).

Annually:
- Change oil in automatic transmission.

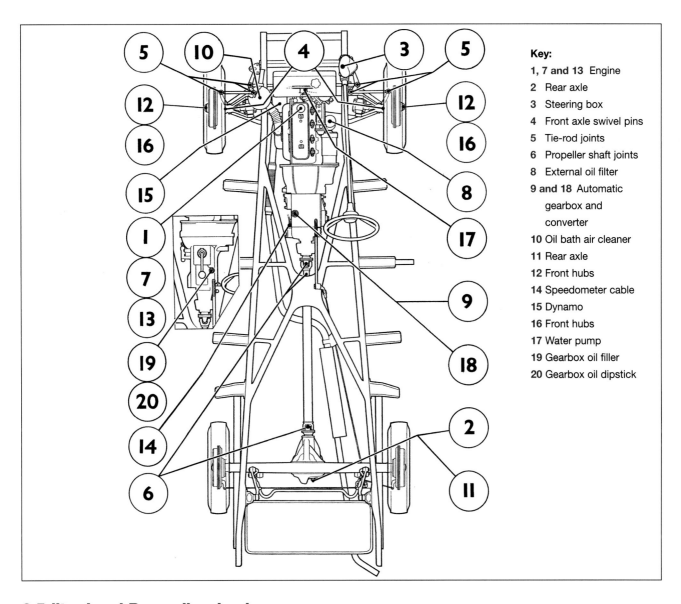

Key:

1, 7 and 13 Engine
2 Rear axle
3 Steering box
4 Front axle swivel pins
5 Tie-rod joints
6 Propeller shaft joints
8 External oil filter
9 and 18 Automatic gearbox and converter
10 Oil bath air cleaner
11 Rear axle
12 Front hubs
14 Speedometer cable
15 Dynamo
16 Front hubs
17 Water pump
19 Gearbox oil filler
20 Gearbox oil dipstick

2.5-litre Land Rover diesel only
Every 50,000 miles:
■ Change timing belt.

Fairway
Every 4,500 miles or 3 months:
■ Change engine oil and filter.
■ Grease all front suspension and steering joints and propshaft universal joints. Adjust front and rear brakes.

Every 9,000 miles:
■ Change fuel filter.

Every 18,000 miles:
■ Replace air filter.
■ Change oil in automatic transmission.

ABOVE The lubrication chart from an early FX4/FL2 workshop manual. Thanks to improved oil and bearing design technology, and changes in specification, this schedule grew less complex and the intervals increased over time, until the service schedule of the Fairway 95 involved the least number of tasks at the widest frequency. *(London Taxi Company/ Author's Collection)*

Fairway Driver
Every 6,000 miles or 3 months:
■ Change engine oil and filter.

Every 12,000 miles or 6 months:
■ Change fuel filter.

Every 18,000 miles:
■ Replace air filter.
■ Change oil in automatic transmission.

Chapter Five

The enthusiast's view

If you want to receive attention from the public outside of any major city, then buy and run an old London taxi. Better still, make it an FX4, the most serviceable of all types you can find.

Many people worldwide have chosen to do so, and have either restored them to original condition or modified them in all manner of ways.

LEFT Two Fairway 95s belonging to members of the London Vintage Taxi Association wait to enter the main ring at the Uxbridge Autoshow in 2010. *(Author)*

ABOVE Just as it is
possible to find the
most remarkable rare
vehicles, early Austins
do turn up in original
if somewhat shabby
condition. This 1960
model is one such cab.
*(SnapdragonFamily
Photography.co.uk)*

Buying an FX4

Mechanically, the FX4 was as well
engineered as any BMC vehicle of its
time, and as straightforward to maintain. This
is why it has survived for so long. The potential
buyer will have choices not offered to a cab
proprietor when the FX4 could be bought new.

All that was available was the single model that
was made at the time with, later on, the option
of some extras, and the choice of buying a
second-hand one, which at times could have
been a less reliable or a more powerful model.
Now, the buyer of a historic vehicle has a wider
choice. The rarest, and also least pleasant, to
drive, is the original 2.2-litre Austin. The 'new
shape' 2.2-litre is a little quieter, but still as slow.
The survival rate of these early cabs is very low.
Although it is not known how many still exist,
the number is not great, partly because of rust
and partly because the classic car world of the
time was not interested in such 'commonplace'
vehicles, as it is today, and they were simply
neglected. A fair number were exported to
America, where some can still be found in
all manner of condition, and sometimes with
rather unusual paint jobs and modifications.
Occasionally, examples are imported back to
the UK. However, these older types are either
for the connoisseur or collector, or for those
who hire them out for film and TV work.

Examples of the 2.5-litre Austin are not
much more common, especially the earlier
ones. However, because the ten-year rule on
licensing in London was relaxed while the later
ones were still in service, and many proprietors
hung on to them rather than buy FX4Rs, a

RIGHT Some earlier
FX4s have been
restored to superb
condition, such as
this 1968 Austin now
owned by a family in
Holland. *(Timon and
Jan Dik)*

higher proportion have survived. A few lasted until 2000, when their owners retired rather than spend £1,500 on having them converted for wheelchair access.

The FX4R, FX4S and S-Plus are rare because they were only made for a comparatively short time. They are, however, better for the enthusiast to drive than the Austins, for the reasons given below. If you are lucky enough to find an FX4R with a 3-litre Perkins engine, and the body is sound, seriously consider buying it, as its performance is the best of all of the early 1980s Carbodies models. Second only in power to the Perkins conversion, but arguably the best replacement engine all round, was the 2.5-litre Nissan. These engines were installed mostly in the FX4S and S-Plus, and some examples of the FX4S were fitted with Fairway and S-Plus interiors. It can be confusing to the buyer to come across any of these, but a check of the VIN ought to confirm which model it is.

For the new owner, who wants a vehicle to drive in modern traffic without too much hassle, and have a slightly better degree of comfort, the best choice is the Fairway series. There are plenty about, for two main reasons. First, they were the last to be built and so are relatively new and, secondly, many of them have only

ABOVE The interior of this very smart FX4S-Plus received a wheelchair conversion immediately prior to 2000. Some owners of older cabs took theirs off the road rather than spend the £1,500 needed to keep them eligible for licensing, but this owner felt it worthwhile for such a good-condition cab. It is now in private hands. *(Murray Jackson)*

BELOW LEFT The Fairway makes a great entry-level vehicle for anyone interested in owning and running old London taxis. This top-condition Fairway Driver has an interesting past. Before it was bought by a London fleet proprietor, it belonged to the British police, or more precisely the National Crime Squad (the forerunner of the Serious Organised Crime Agency), which used it for surveillance work. Vehicles used on this job were known as 'Charlie Browns'. Why, it is not clear, but possibly the name was derived from the dog belonging to Charlie Brown in Charles M. Schultz's 'Peanuts' cartoons, whose name was of course, 'Snoopy'. *(Ceejay Autos)*

recently come off the road. In fact, at the time of writing, there were still quite a few in service in London and they could be bought from various operators when they were retired. The condition of these varied enormously. Some were so worn out and rusty they were only fit for spares, whereas others had been kept tidy and made fairly straightforward running restoration projects. Others were very well maintained and a few were in impeccable condition. A fair number of those in private hands have been renovated or even fully restored, while some have been re-trimmed to a luxurious level for the wedding market.

The FX4R and the FX4Q, which used an Indian-made version of the 2.5-litre Austin diesel and, in early examples at least, a number of reconditioned mechanical components, both had a reputation for unreliability. What should be remembered, though, is that a cab in private hands will do fewer miles in a year than a working cab would in a couple of months. So what was not tough enough for the kind of hard work that a London taxi has to do, might be perfectly adequate for the light mileage that an enthusiast may give a cab. That is, of course, unless you plan a round-the-world trip, and then you need to find the best version you can in the best condition you can, and make sure

everything is properly overhauled before you start out!

Wear and tear will have taken its toll on the best looked-after cab. It will have been driven for at least 100 miles a day for almost every day of its life, which can be at least ten years and will have had its doors, seats and windows used literally thousands of times. The passenger door alone will have been opened at least 25,000 times! Many of the ancillaries, such as the radiator, the brake servo, the alternator and the starter motor will have been changed at least once, if not several times, and the bodywork repaired, because of either rust or damage incurred in an accident. Thus, however good it looks, it is still a vehicle that has had a lot of use. It's what it was bought for!

There are a number of options for acquiring a retired FX4. You can buy from a private individual, be he a member of the London Vintage Taxi Association or a vendor on eBay (or both!), a cab driver or cab fleet proprietor who is selling a Fairway out of service, or one of a small number of specialist dealers. Whoever you buy from, what condition you may find the cab in will depend very much on who the last owner was. If you buy out of service, it may well be bought 'as seen', with or without an MoT certificate. Some proprietors selling cabs have brought them up

RIGHT FX4s have fans all over the world. Crazy Cabs of Paris was formed by restaurateur Jean-Pierre Milan, and survives to this day. The club's base was La Closerie des Lilas on the Boulevarde Montparnasse, the famous restaurant and haunt of such celebrities as Ernest Hemingway, which Milan owned. *(London Vintage Taxi Association Archive)*

to a reasonable condition, and got an MoT on them, but this is not always the case. This can be a good way to buy, because the owner will be able to tell you what has been replaced and what might need doing in due course.

Older FX4s bought from private owners can vary vastly in condition. They might be barn finds, partially restored or fully restored, in which case it is a matter of *caveat emptor*, 'buyer beware'. The cab may have had a lot of work done on it, or very little. 'Barn finds' can be very rusty indeed, and be fit only for spares. Whoever you buy from, it is all the more important that you take someone along with you who knows what they are looking at. If the buyer is extremely lucky, the cab may be totally original and very sound, but although finds like this do happen, such instances are very rare indeed.

Buying a Fairway from a dealer

Most of the FX4s bought from dealers these days will be Fairways. Although older FX4s are bought up, these are often those sold to the USA and mainland Europe during the 1970s and 1980s, and since re-imported. These will most likely be sold 'as seen'. If you buy a renovated Fairway from a dealer, it may well come with an MoT and may look very smart, with the bodywork tidied up, run well and be ready to drive away and enjoy. This does not mean that you will not have to spend any money on it at some time in the future. Remember the mileage it will have done and minor components may be a few years old and might soon wear out. For the price you will pay, the dealer will do what is necessary to get it through the MoT, rather than overhaul everything in sight. He will work on the principle of 'if it ain't broke, I ain't gonna mend it'.

Although he will have to weld any rust spots on places like the sills, which compromise the structural soundness of the body to get it through the MoT, he will repair the bottoms of the doors, and other visible, non-structural places on the body with filler, just as a cab garage would do for its annual licensing. For the price he is charging you, it is not worth his while to repair these visible body panels with new metal. There will be no warranty on the

vehicle, implied or otherwise. Such warranties on older vehicles are supplied by insurance companies and are not a viable proposition for an old FX4. For the dealer there simply is not the profit in the deal to underwrite one himself. If the differential or gearbox gives out on you two months after buying the cab, then that's tough luck. However, if there is, for instance, a brake

LEFT Because Fairways have been kept in service for longer than any previous FX4 model, they stand to have more rust. Serious problems like this rust on the front axle beam of a Fairway Driver, if not spotted at a pre MoT inspection, can mean expensive repair bills. *(Author)*

BELOW Sills are structural to the body, and can rot badly over time. Either be aware that they need repairing and be prepared to spend money and time in getting them fixed, or make sure you buy a cab that has had this job, and other major bodywork, done properly, and that the price you pay for the cab is appropriate for its condition. *(Author)*

failure a couple of days after you've got the cab home, and the MoT is new, then the dealer might repair that damage out of goodwill, but that would be up to him entirely.

One piece of advice that cannot be stressed enough is that you should always buy the best example you can possibly afford, and if you can't afford it, don't buy it. Don't let your dreams run away with you, or listen too much to, or read too much into, the seller's spiel. With an FX4, the best has to mean the soundest bodywork, because repairing rust can, and often will, take up a huge amount of your time and money.

Importing an FX4

One word of caution about buying a retired FX4 if you are not a resident of the UK. If you want to import it into your own country, do check first with the authorities to make sure you are allowed to do so; find out what taxes you might be liable for, and whether you are even allowed to use it. In the USA, for instance, a vehicle under 25 years old may not be imported unless it has been modified to meet the existing safety and exhaust emission regulations, which rules out, at the time of writing, anything newer

than most of the Rover models. Holland allows the import of old vehicles, but exemptions for the equivalent of the road fund licence do not come in until the vehicle is more than 25 years old. Certain states in Germany actually forbid the use of older vehicles, especially those with diesel engines.

What to look for when buying an FX4

Engines

With the exception of the FX4R, the diesel engines fitted to FX4s were well proven and long lived. There is not much different to look for in any of these engines that you wouldn't check on a petrol engine. Look for oil and water leaks, piston ring blow-by through the oil filler, and generally excessive mechanical noise. This last point is more difficult for the inexperienced to identify, as the 'knock' of the diesel engine will tend to obscure anything else, but as the engine settles to a tick-over, it should be free of anything above the rattle of the combustion. The engine should rev freely, even if it seems a bit slower to do so than a petrol engine, and

there should be no oil smoke or excessive black exhaust. (If you rev the engine to its maximum, there will be some black smoke, as a result of 'overfuelling', the process by which an injector pump delivers a larger amount of fuel in order to increase revs and power.)

If you can smell diesel fuel when you open the bonnet, make sure you can locate the source of any leak. If it comes from one of the external pipes or the lift pump, these are not difficult or expensive to replace, but if it seems to come from the injector pump, be wary as this is a pricey piece of kit to repair or replace.

If the owner starts the engine with a can of spray starter fluid, be very suspicious. It is true that the fuel in any motor vehicle that has been left standing will have deteriorated and will therefore be less effective in starting the car, but use of this 'wonder spray' may hide worn-out injectors (not a massive expense to replace), a worn injector pump (which, as we've just said, is expensive), or worn cylinder bores (even more expensive).

A lot of Austin diesels will have done at least a quarter of a million miles in service, plus more in private hands. The cylinder head can become so firmly fixed to the block that it is impossible

to remove it without actually breaking the surface of the head from the rest of the casting. If the cab you are offered has an engine in poor condition, it is best to leave it alone unless you have another one, ready overhauled or in preparation, to install.

Automatic gearboxes

Automatic gearboxes should change up and down smoothly and should not leak. Gears should engage promptly without any excessive 'clunk'. Repairing them is an expert job and it can be expensive if major work needs to be done. The Borg-Warner DG150M automatic gearbox, fitted up to 1964 was, in itself, a superb piece of engineering, but an FX4 that still has one will be very rare indeed these days. The BW35, BW65, BW66 and BW40 automatic boxes that were variously used from 1962 to 1988 proved to be more suitable, and the 2.5-litre Austin and 2.5-litre Land Rover diesel engines both had sufficient power to work with automatic transmissions. The 2.3-litre Land Rover diesel, however, struggled with an automatic box, especially if the cab was fitted with power steering, which further drained power from the engine.

ABOVE The engine compartment of this 1970 Austin would not win any prizes at a concours event, but it is clean and shows no sign of any fuel, oil or water leaks, which is vital for any motor vehicle. *(Author)*

An FX4R automatic without power steering, which was optional until early 1983, is a slightly livelier performer. The Jatco automatic transmission fitted to the Nissan is as tough and reliable as the Nissan engine and, provided the Pierburg valve that controls the gearchange on later models is in good condition, it will change up and down smoothly. If the Pierburg valve is faulty it will cause the gearbox to 'hover' between upward changes and delay engaging the gear when kicked down. It is an external component and is not difficult to replace.

Manual gearboxes

The Austin manual gearbox was also well designed and, if heavy, was smooth to use and reliable. It was a standard BMC commercial unit so beware of the usual problems, like jumping out of gear on overrun and, of course, oil leaks, especially from around the join between the bellhousing and the engine block. This could mean that, if it is clear gear oil and not black engine oil, the input shaft bearing oil seal needs replacing. This means that the gearbox has to come out. Naturally, if the engine rear main bearing oil seal has gone, the gearbox will have to come out to enable you to fix that too. Incidentally, that old problem of BMC gearboxes, worn synchromesh on second gear, seemed not to be a thing that affected these gearboxes.

The real issue with driving a manual Austin, as has been said before, is the heaviness of the clutch. But having said that, if the cab is not used constantly in town traffic, it is bearable, provided you don't suffer from knee problems. The Rover five-speed manual in the FX4R, FX4S and FX4S-Plus is a smooth, modern unit with a clutch as light as a car's, which of course it is! Early problems were that the input shaft bearing was the wrong type and would collapse, causing the gearbox to destroy itself. If the cab has lasted this long, then it has been fitted with the right bearing and, in light private use, ought not to give trouble. Another early problem with the FX4R was the clutch actuating arm. This is a steel stamping, clipped on to a ball mounting. Within a very short time, the vibration of the engine, especially if a driver kept his foot on the clutch at traffic lights in an attempt to quell the rattle the clutch bearing produced, would wear a hole right through the actuating arm, giving the appearance that a large bullet had been fired through it. Again, if an FX4R has survived this long, then the problem has been remedied. The Nissan five-speed manual gearbox fitted to the Fairway range is as tough as the engine and the automatic transmission.

Front suspension and steering

The front suspension and steering on models up to 1992 was of a standard pattern as used on BMC cars of the time. Kingpins can be, and often were, incorrectly fitted, which made the steering excessively stiff. It will feel heavier than most older cars that do not have power steering, but it should not feel stiff at any speed, and should return to a straight ahead position of its own accord. If it feels stiff then the kingpins need to be stripped and assembled properly, and most likely rebuilt as well. Neglecting basic lubrication will cause the kingpins and fulcrum pins to wear excessively, making the steering dangerously loose and adversely affecting the suspension, so if an FX4 older than a Fairway Driver tends to wander excessively then the chances are that the front suspension is shot and needs rebuilding. Badly assembled kingpins will also cause excessive wear in the wishbone rubbers.

Rebuilding the steering and suspension assembly is not a hugely expensive job and can be carried out by the average amateur mechanic with little difficulty. The suspension on the Fairway Driver and Fairway 95 is of a more simple type with ball joints, and easier to maintain and overhaul.

Back axle and suspension

The back axle on most models was a Salisbury type. It is robust and quiet and, if treated properly, lasts for quite a high mileage. That large, empty-looking passenger compartment can act as an echo chamber, so it can make you think that the differential is noisy, but a worn back axle will make its presence known by a very distinct whine. Overhauling a worn one requires the kind of skill not normally taught in technical colleges these days, but nevertheless can be done by someone with experience of this type of axle. The later GKN axle, supplied to the Fairway Driver is slightly less robust but has proved perfectly adequate for the job required of it, so unless it has been badly treated, will serve the enthusiast very well.

Brakes

The drum brakes fitted from 1958 to 1992 are quite simple in their construction and not overly expensive to maintain and overhaul. The pedals on Austins are mounted on a shaft under the floor, which needs regular greasing. This can either seize or it can become worn, causing the pedal to feel loose on the shaft. Repair, which involves re-bushing, is simple. Ageing wheel cylinders are prone to leak as the rubbers deteriorate, and the mechanism can seize up. The servo fitted from 1980 can leak air, and the dashboard warning light on the S-Plus and Fairway can indicate that it is not working properly. Do check, however that the rubber hoses connecting the servo pump to the servo have not perished and are letting in air.

On all Austins fitted with a brake servo, and the FX4R and FX4Q, there is a brake servo pump. This is fitted because there is no butterfly in the inlet manifold to create a vacuum, and the pump fulfils this task. The brackets on which the pump was mounted were notorious for cracking, so check to see that they are sound. (The build quality of these brackets was very inconsistent: some lasted for the life of the cab, while others broke within months.) Other problems with the brakes are the normal ones you would expect. Watch for them pulling to

one side; for a handbrake lever that comes up too high, and for general ineffectiveness. The discs and callipers on Fairway Drivers are also simple to maintain. The rear drums on these models have self-adjusting shoes.

Electrical components

The electrical components and the wiring are all straightforward but, of course, the wiring on the older models may have perished. If you are restoring an early example, especially one that has not been used for a while, you might have to consider a complete rewire. On any older

ABOVE The pinion oil seal will leak in time, making a real mess of the diff casing. Removal and replacement is straightforward, providing it is done properly. The noise from a worn diff is accentuated by the sheer size of a cab's interior. *(Jimmy Waters)*

BELOW The heater box is located on top of the scuttle, under the bonnet. In time the matrix becomes clogged with silt and will need renovation if you want your FX4 to be comfortable to drive in all weathers. The flap at the bottom controls the direction of air, either to the driver's feet or to the windscreen, and the spring that holds it open or closed can break, preventing air from blowing on the windscreen. *(Jimmy Waters)*

vehicle, earth connections will deteriorate as damp corrodes the two surfaces, so any apparently faulty malfunctioning equipment, such as brake lights flashing or rear lights going off when the brake pedal is pressed, might be caused by nothing more complicated than a bad earth.

Bodywork

The real bugbear for the trade with older FX4s was, and will continue to be for the enthusiast, rust. Sills suffer badly from this, being exposed to the elements and are a lengthy job to replace. Both inner and outer sills can rust badly, as can the bottoms of the door pillars, where the sills attach. On Fairways in particular, because of the extended life that most had, the rear wheel arches and boot floor can rust out and it is an extensive and costly job to repair or replace these parts. Front wings are also very prone to rust, as the seams between inner and outer panels and around the headlights harbour dirt and moisture, and these will rot out over the years. New steel front wings are all but impossible to obtain, and there are several different types, depending on the model. Glassfibre wings have been available for some time and although the earlier ones were a poor fit, the latest versions are of reasonably good quality and have actually been approved for use on working cabs in London.

Over the years, rust can attack the scuttle, with telltale signs of it close to the bottom of the windscreen pillars. If it is seen here, it can be repaired fairly easily, but may not be detected in out-of-sight places until these parts, which are structural to the body, have been affected extensively. These are particularly expensive and difficult to replace and, considering the modest value of even the best FX4s, makes restoration an unviable proposition.

Fairways, despite having better protection than earlier models, can be affected by rust far worse than older Austins. This is because the PCO had relaxed their ten-year rule some time before and thus the cabs were kept in service for far longer, often twice as long as the Austins were in the 1960s and 1970s, and thus were exposed to the elements for far

ABOVE Rust like this on the scuttle and bonnet is common and not serious. Much worse is rust underneath and inside the scuttle. *(Author)*

RIGHT Rust will form around the headlight and along the join between the inner and, outer front wings and in service, the damage would be repaired with filler. These are not structural, but new-old-stock steel panels are no longer available. *(Author)*

RIGHT The boot floor and spare wheel well can rust out over time. Depending on the extent, this can be repaired with this 'triple panel', consisting of the spare wheel well and boot floor pressings. *(Dave Cooper)*

longer. Chassis rot can be found on Fairways, usually on the front section. The housings for the coil springs on Fairway Drivers can also harbour mud and moisture, causing these to rot through. Having said that, some proprietors spent time and money keeping these older cabs on the road, rather than spend out on a less trustworthy TXII, and thus it is worth looking closely at retired Fairways to see just what has and has not been done in the way of rust repair.

Interior fittings

The interior is simple, with plastic mouldings covering all the doors, although these are prone to splitting. A dull finish can be revived with a good proprietary cleaning product. The leather on the pre-1969 models does wear, but it is durable and in many cases can be revived with proprietary products. The headlining, like on all cars, is difficult to replace and unless it has been torn, it will probably be serviceable.

Supplementary exhaust fittings

If you are buying, or have recently bought, a Fairway or Fairway Driver that has been licensed in London in the past four years, it will have had some equipment fitted which brings its exhaust emissions up to Euro 3 standard. This will have been fitted in accordance with Public Carriage Office requirements, not through national or European law. It will be one of two types: the Van Aaken recirculating equipment or the STT Emtec turbocharger. Although adherents of the turbocharger swear by the additional performance it gives the cab, it was debatable whether it was wise to fit a turbocharger on an engine that had already done at least 300,000 miles.

The Van Aaken system can go off-tune, and you would need the software for your laptop, and a set of leads to connect up the control systems in order to retune it. As the cab will perform adequately, or in most cases better without it, it is better to take the cab to a taxi specialist, preferably one who had fitted the equipment, and have it removed and a new exhaust system fitted. The Van Aaken equipment requires a catalytic

converter to work properly, whereas the cab originally did not have one. It is perfectly legal to run a Fairway as a private vehicle without the Van Aaken or STT Emtec equipment, as its fitting was solely a requirement laid down by the PCO.

It is simple to remove both pieces of equipment, but do consult a taxi specialist before doing so if you are uncertain about what's involved. Removing either system is only illegal if you are still licensing your Fairway as a taxi in London. In any case, you will not be able to do this if it is 15 years old or more anyway, but as a private vehicle you will be returning it to its original specification. What is more, with the Van Aaken system, the performance will be improved and stay better, so long as the engine remains in good condition.

Air conditioning

Some Fairways were fitted with air conditioning, for the driver only. This is nice to have, of course, but do follow the maker's instructions regarding its servicing. If it is faulty, and it looks like you might be facing hefty bills to have it repaired or replaced, consider removing it, as it is only a bolt-on system and the cab will work perfectly well without such equipment. Air conditioning units contain potentially hazardous refrigerants, so consult your local authority about safe, legal disposal.

ABOVE The rear wheel arches rust out over time, necessitating either extensive patching or a complete replacement of the panels. *(Author)*

ABOVE Driving an earlier FX4 is a much better experience if the cab is fully restored, like this Belgian-owned 1980 model. *(Carl Despriet)*

RIGHT This is what faces you when you get behind the wheel of a 2.5-litre FX4. An FX4R and FX4Q would be similar, except that the gearchange lever would be mounted on the floor rather than on the steering column. *(Author)*

What are they like to drive?

Now that you know a little about the different types you can buy, you may wonder what it is like to sit in that driver's seat and have the kind of view that a London cabbie has every working day. The viewpoint is the same for all models, but that is certainly not true for how they drive. One thing is common to all, however, and that is that squeaks and rattles from the body, and the draughts and water leaks are inherent. Some say they are part of the cab's character. With a commercial diesel engine, be it the oldest Austin or a more recent Nissan, which is installed in a vehicle with simple 1950s technology, there will always be some level of noise. If you want Rolls-Royce silence and comfort, then buy a Rolls-Royce. The FX4 is not for you.

General impressions

The first thing you notice when you get into an FX4 is the high, upright driving position, and that substantial (usually) black bonnet stretching out in front. This seating position gives a great view of the traffic and when you experience it you can understand one of the reasons why taxi drivers in London pilot their cabs so confidently around the streets. The other reason of course is that because they have 'done The Knowledge', they know exactly where they are going!

Another thing you immediately notice is how little room you have. The lack of room is more apparent in pre-1969 models, but nevertheless, the amount in subsequent models is not much greater. This is because the cab was designed when people were smaller than they are now. In fact, the leg and headroom dimensions of the first FX4s is identical to that of the previous model, the FX3, which was designed in the 1940s. The people who would be driving the first FX4s were born before the benefits of the Welfare State and increased prosperity of the post-war years had had time to exert their influence on the population. Those born after the Second World War grew taller, and needed more legroom and headroom, especially when peering out of that letter box-sized windscreen.

Firing up

Now that you're sitting in the cab, fire up the engine. If it's an Austin or an FX4R, turn the start key over to the first position, so as to give the heater plugs about 30 seconds to warm up, then, push in the stop knob (this will happen automatically on an FX4R when you turn the starter key), and operate the starter. After a few turns, the engine will begin to fire and gradually roar into life, settling down to a tractor-like chugging idle. Get used to this level of noise: it will be your constant companion all the time you drive the cab. An FX4S and S-Plus will fire up without the need for heater plugs, and the noise will be a bit more subdued, but it will still be there.

Much more civilised is the Fairway. Turn the key to the first position, wait for the little orange light on the dashboard by the driver's door to go out, and then turn the key further to start the engine. The chirrup of the Japanese-made starter tells you this is different, but the noise level, although still noticeable, is lower. The sound, accompanied by the whine of the viscous fan is a much smoother one.

Going for a test drive

Let's imagine you are in an Austin. Diesels of this vintage are notoriously gutless when cold,

BELOW London Taxi Exports built this cabriolet conversion of a Fairway Driver, which was built for the leader of a West African country. It has a separate panel in the roof to allow the leader to stand and wave at the crowds. (*London Taxi Exports*)

so let the engine warm up for a minute or two. If you are in a 2.2-litre cab with a manual gearbox, and you are on level ground you can select second gear to pull away, because first is so low you will need to change up after about 5mph (8kph). That is, after you've got over the shock of discovering how heavy that clutch is! If you are in a 2.5-litre Austin, take notice of that little red and white sign on the dash that tells you to engage first gear from rest. This cab has a higher-ratio differential, so you'll either bog the engine down if you don't give it a lot of loud pedal (it's far more difficult to stall a diesel engine than a petrol, although not impossible) or you'll burn the clutch out if you make a habit of slipping it in too high a gear.

Now pull away. No, there's nothing wrong with the steering, or your arms. It really is that heavy. Take it easy for now, as you'll be surprised at how much effort you need to put into driving this beast, and how low-geared the steering is. Now get up to speed. In a 2.2-litre Austin, expect to cruise at no more than 45mph (about 70kph) on the open road, but don't expect to have in-depth conversations with anyone sitting on the back seat; you will not be able to hear them unless they sit on the tip-up seat and talk through the gap in the partition glass! If you are in a post-1969 model, you could take out the piece of wood that prevents the glass from sliding open more than four inches, but that will only help a little. (A lot of private owners, especially in the USA, remove the glass altogether.)

An early petrol cab or FL2 Hire Car will have slightly better performance and the noise level will be lower, and of course in an FL2 you will have a seat in the front for a passenger to keep you company. (Private owners may have fitted a second front seat to an FX4.) The 2.5-litre Austins offer better acceleration, but not by any great degree, although the extra power is sufficient to make an automatic model viable. The automatic transmission became a more popular option as the 1970s went on, and as a result the manual transmission models were bought less and less.

Cabs with Land Rover engines are a bit different. The 2.3-litre diesel automatic is as slow getting away as the 2.2-litre Austin. If you want the performance to be a tad more lively,

change gear manually using the 'Low' and 'D' positions on the selector. The Land Rover engine will rev more freely than the Austin, and to about 1,000rpm higher. The FX4S and Plus accelerate a bit like the 2.5-litre Austin, which is not startling, but at least adequate for modern town traffic. The difference between the Austins and the models with Rover engines is in the steering and the brakes, which are power-assisted and give a feel like a modern Transit van. The manual gearbox will allow a slightly brisker getaway, and the clutch is far lighter too, as it is the same as the one fitted to the Rover SD1. The FX4R, when new was almost eerily quiet, but as these engines piled on the mileage, they got noisier. The acceleration of the automatic model is poor and that of the manual is not much better, but the top speed is alarmingly high.

The best drive of all is without doubt the Fairway. As with the other models, give it a minute or two to warm up when starting from cold, especially on a cold day, and also to let the oil circulate around the power steering box. The chances are that you will be in an automatic, as they were the most popular choice in London. Select drive (or reverse, if the way you're facing demands it!) give it a reasonable amount of throttle, and off you go. OK, so it's not a BMW, but in comparison with the old Austins, it almost could be! The noise level is acceptable, if not up to 21st century car standards, but this is a working vehicle and it is far better to compare it with the aforementioned Transit van.

Visibility

For a vehicle that was considered by the toughest taxi licensing authority in the world to be safe, and for one that gave the driver such a commanding view of the traffic, the FX4 paradoxically has a number of blind spots. The most obvious is the shallow windscreen, especially for a tall driver, who is obliged to drive with his head bent forward, or have the seat set so low as to cause back problems if he drives for too long. Another obstruction is the thickness of the windscreen pillars and the top corner of the pillar, which can and does obscure visibility to the right. Care must be taken, at pedestrian crossings in particular, to make sure you do

not run anyone over simply because you have failed to see them. Another obstruction is the taximeter, if fitted to the B-post. This can make pulling out of a side road tricky, so be doubly sure the road is clear when doing so, especially if you are driving an older, 2.2-litre model that will accelerate at a somewhat modest speed in front of the traffic that will very quickly catch you up!

Condensation on windows is a problem that occurs on all motor vehicles. It is, however, more of a problem with an FX4. The demisters on all models, even the Fairway, are nowhere near as effective as on modern cars. This is compounded by the fact that the driver is in a much more confined space, so it is wise to keep a chamois leather or similar in the front of the cab to keep the screen and the side windows clear. For the same reason, the glass in the partition can steam up as well, causing further difficulties.

Using your FX4

The FX4's classic shape makes it popular as a wedding car. The smooth engine and smart interior of the Fairway, and the modern running gear of the Fairway Driver, makes them more reliable and quieter than older vehicles. Some have been re-sprayed white, and others have had extensive work done to the interiors to really make the bride feel pampered.

Film and TV work is available for the owners of older cabs (and has been until recently, for Fairways, for the making of contemporary TV dramas such as *Spooks* or *Hustle*), but it is a

specialist job and not one that every enthusiast feels comfortable doing. It can involve many hours waiting around for the director to call the driver to do his job and the money is not always good, as film and TV production

The Hertz London Taxi Marathon

1981 was declared The International Year of the Disabled. Steve Tillyer, the assistant editor of *Cab Driver* newspaper decided he would raise funds for a related cause, and set a new world record for a taxi fare in the process. He had acquired a new Austin FX4 through Hertz's newly introduced lease-hire scheme, and through his newspaper connections, persuaded Hertz to be the main sponsors for the trip.

Hertz had the cab painted in their trademark yellow colour and paid for its running throughout the journey. Further help came from one of the London cab trade's oldest charities, The London Taxi Drivers' Fund for Underprivileged Children. They, along with Hertz, chose the Whitefield School in Walthamstow, a special needs school, as the recipients of the money collected. A sunshine roof and a top-tinted windscreen were fitted and James Putnam, whose company was making and supplying orthopaedic seats for FX4s, donated one which, said Steve, made the journey far more comfortable. Andrew Overton, managing director of Mann & Overton, provided a sealed box of spares for the trip, which, incidentally, were never needed. The PCO checked over the cab and tested the brake fluid to see if it was good enough for the high altitudes that Steve would encounter in the Alps.

To make it a proper 'job', Steve needed a passenger and volunteered his brother, Ray. The run began when Ray hailed Steve at Marble Arch on 21 September. The meter was kept running the whole time, and this would be the target figure for the sponsorship money raised. Steve and Ray visited Hertz's offices in ten countries and returned to the Hertz office in Marble Arch on 18 October, six weeks and 7,500 road miles later.

The trip raised just under £10,000, which was very close to the amount shown on the taximeter and provided a substantial part of the cost of a new hydrotherapy pool for Whitefield School. It was opened by the then MP for Chingford, the Rt Hon. Norman Tebbit, now Baron Tebbit of Chingford, who himself had connections with the school.

ABOVE In the sponsor's distinctive yellow colour, the Marathon Austin FX4 poses on Westminster Bridge, with that other icon of London's transport, a Routemaster bus. *(Steve Tillyer)*

RIGHT The Hertz Taxi Marathon cab, with Steve Tillyer at the wheel. *(Steve Tillyer)*

ABOVE Very exciting is this 1979 Austin, with an 8.2-litre Chevrolet V8, producing 450bhp. It has a 0–60 time of 4.3 seconds and covers the quarter-mile in 11.8 seconds. It has full hydraulic suspension that can make it 'dance'. Needless to say, it has been built by a very skilled engineer. *(Steve Birchall)*

ABOVE The 18in-wide rear wheels only allow space for one passenger. At least the TV and 1,000-watt sound system make up for the lack of company. *(Steve Birchall)*

companies are feeling the pinch as much as anybody. If you've never done this type of work before, think carefully before you embark on it. If you've done it with other vehicles, then an older cab may be another useful vehicle to add to your fleet.

FX4s restored to their original condition are quite rare, partly because the actual numbers of surviving earlier models are small in themselves. Many in the USA have had some conversion work on them, including the fitting of different engines and air conditioning. Such work requires specialist knowledge and the installation of a larger, more powerful engine in an FX4 without changing the brakes to a more powerful system can be highly dangerous. Unless you are someone with that ability and have the facilities, leave the cab in its original specification.

The availability of spare parts and the simplicity of repair make them ideal enthusiasts' vehicles and many have been used for promotional purposes. Others have been converted into vans or pickups, although it has to be said, the workmanship of some of the earlier examples was very rough and ready.

A lot of preserved FX4s, however, are owned for the sheer pleasure of having such a special vehicle; one that always attracts attention – and that is the way it should be.

ABOVE Some early FX4s were converted to pickup trucks. Most were crude, but an exception is this Fairway, built by Mick Gibbon of Mann & Overton. This photograph was taken at the Taxi Driver of the Year Show at Battersea Park. *(London Vintage Taxi Association Archive)*

LEFT The FX4 is always an eye-catcher, and all the more so when used by another of London's legends, the Pearly Kings and Queens. This Fairway belongs to Alf Dole, the Pearly King of St Pancras. *(Mark Cooper)*

Epilogue

There is not much room for nostalgia in business, but after years of at least tolerating, if not outright deriding, the FX4, London's cab trade will miss its final version, the Fairway. Not for its rattles, squeaks and leaks, but because it was cheaper to run than a TX1 and more reliable than either a TXII or TX4. The FX4 has always had its enthusiasts, and always will; people who love its shape and its character, who have lovingly maintained the ones they own, and enjoy the attention such a distinctive vehicle attracts.

Whatever London has decided, the world is still enjoying its most famous and most recognisable taxi, the FX4.

LEFT Manganese Bronze CEO John Russell offers trade-in deals for Fairways against new TX4s. *(London Taxi Company)*

Appendix 1

The Conditions of Fitness and the Public Carriage Office

London's taxis are different from those of any other capital city because of a set of regulations called the Conditions of Fitness for Motor Cabs. These are written by the licensing authority, the Public Carriage Office, and date back to May 1906. There had been rules for London's horse cabs for centuries, and these governed such things as their state of repair, and the size and number of horses required to pull them. In the early years of the 20th century, motor cars of any type were still new, and few people knew much about them, including the senior officer at the PCO, Chief Inspector Arthur Bassom. His brief was the safety of the travelling public, so with the consent of his superior officer, he and his assistant, Sub-divisional Inspector Beckley, took a course on motor mechanics and driving, so as not to be 'at the mercy of every profession that professes knowledge'. He consulted Lord Montagu of Beaulieu (the father of the present holder of that title), who recommended W. Worby Beaumont, author of *Motor Vehicles and Motors: their Design, Construction and Working by Steam, Oil and Electricity*, to frame the first Conditions of Fitness for Motor Cabs.

A point of great controversy from the very outset was the 25ft turning circle. The fledgling motor industry complained bitterly at this bar to their entry to what they had envisaged would be a lucrative market. At the time, there were 11,000-odd horse cabs in London. To supply even 10 per cent of that number would represent a great amount of business at a time when weekly production was measured in, at best, dozens. It would be impossible, they said, to adapt an existing model to comply with this rule. Nevertheless, more than forty makes of cab were type-approved before the Great War.

The Great War reduced the number of cabs on the road, and it was not until late 1919 that the first new model, the Beardmore, appeared. Even then it had to comply with the same Conditions of Fitness that had been laid down in 1906. A further rule that made manufacture difficult in the 1920s was the insistence of a ground clearance of 10in. By the late 1920s, the motor car had changed beyond all recognition from its horseless carriage origins, whereas the London taxi still looked like an Edwardian town carriage.

The trade pressed the government for a change in the rules, but Arthur Bassom, now a chief inspector, was engaged in other police projects outside the cab trade, and he spared little time, if any, for the PCO and the Conditions of Fitness. This caused a crisis because, by the middle of the decade, a mere four makes were approved, and only one of those, the Beardmore, was readily available. Eventually, in 1928, the permitted ground clearance was altered to 7in, although the turning circle would remain unchanged.

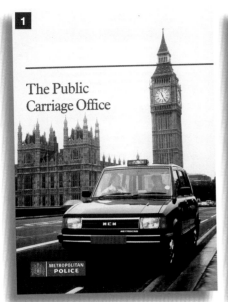

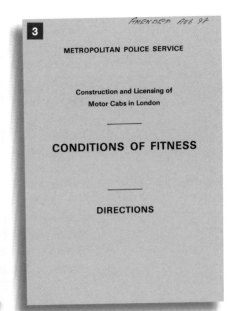

Four new models appeared, from Morris-Commercial, Beardmore, the London General Cab Company (which developed a Citroën cab to their own design), and the most significant of all, the Austin 12/4, commissioned from Austin by Mann & Overton, and the forerunner of the FX4.

Even then, cabmen had to do without the weather protection that was commonplace on contemporary cars. Those in positions of authority thought that closing him in would make him drowsy (although it seems that there were no thoughts in the authority's mind of hypothermia affecting cabmen!) and another consideration, arrived at from practical experience, was that a full windscreen would obscure his vision in London's notorious fogs. Even the trade further entrenched this backward thinking, but in this instance for rather suspect reasons. The landaulette hood, once *de rigueur* on Edwardian town carriages, was losing favour during the 1930s, surviving only on stately limousines, but the cab trade clung to them. Why? 'Ladies of the night' and others on dubious trysts would use the privacy of fully enclosed cabs to pursue their activities, and paid handsomely for the privilege. Only after the Second World War did the PCO ban the landaulette body and cabs began to take on a shape closer to that of existing saloon cars.

Although the Conditions of Fitness were progressively relaxed to accommodate changes in car design and technology, it was not until

1961 that these rules received another major challenge. It came, not from within the trade or the government, but from the advent of the minicab. This form of transport was an offshoot of the long-established private-hire trade which, by and large, had existed peaceably alongside the taxi trade since the earliest years. Now, as Britain grew more prosperous, some private-hire company owners saw a way of cashing in on the growing demand for taxis. They would use telephone bookings, dispatched to the cars by a fairly new innovation in either taxis or private hire: two-way radio.

Although not the first man to introduce minicabs, Michael Gotla, the proprietor of Welbeck Motors, became the most notorious. Private-hire drivers are not allowed by law to

ABOVE AND BELOW

Selection of Public Carriage Office booklets

1 The Public Carriage Office Code of Practice
2 Booklet, *Becoming a licensed taxi driver in London*
3 The Conditions of Fitness
4 Leaflet, *Taxis, Diesel and You*
5 Public Carriage Office general information brochure

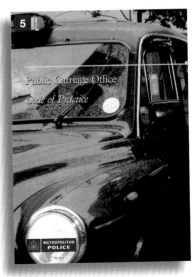

pick up off the street or taxi rank like a taxi driver can, but Gotla instructed his drivers, if approached on the street by a potential passenger, to radio in the booking, which would be relayed to another car. In practice, the driver simply took the passenger and radioed the job to the controller to 'validate' it. The cab trade was up in arms, and serious disorder on the streets occurred when taxi drivers physically, and occasionally violently, tried to prevent minicab drivers from taking work in this way.

Although the taxi trade lobbied hard to get the government to ban minicabs outright, the Home Office took a completely different stance and set up a committee of inquiry to see if purpose-built taxis were really necessary in the first place. After more than a year of deliberation, the committee came down in favour of purpose-built taxis, making just one change, that the requirement for a separate chassis be removed.

The rules remained in place for another half-century, until the builders of so-called 'alternative' vehicles put down a challenge to the turning circle rule. They had seen the opposition in the provincial trade to LTI's imposition of the Fairway and, later the TX-series, and wanted to offer the trade a choice of vehicle that would provide wheelchair accessibility and driver protection that would be cheaper to buy and run. The proponents' models, based on the Fiat Scudo and the virtually identical Peugeot vans, lacked the turning circle, but many provincial licensing authorities were persuaded that this facility was unnecessary in their areas. The vehicles proved very popular and the makers decided to try to enter the London market. After deliberation, the PCO decided that the turning circle was essential for London and, following a judicial review and even longer and very deep scrutiny, the PCO again, in 2005, found in favour of the status quo.

The Public Carriage Office

The prime reason why London's taxi trade and its drivers are consistently voted number one in the world is the power of the licensing authority. Now known as Transport for London Taxis and Private Hire (TPH), this body had been known since 1843 as the Public Carriage Office. It had been set up as a part of the Metropolitan Police, based at their headquarters at Scotland Yard. Even today, old-time cabmen still refer to the PCO as 'The Yard'.

The PCO's primary responsibility was the safety of the travelling public and is TPH's today. This they did by ensuring that all cabs were properly maintained and that cab drivers were fit and proper persons to be entrusted with the job, with neither a criminal record nor a serious health problem.

In the days of horse cabs, the vehicles and horses were subject to annual inspections at Scotland Yard or at one of a large number of places around London, often in the open air and in public view. Following the appearance of London's first motor cab in 1903, a huge variety of vehicles were put forward for approval, and the knowledge required by the officers to inspect and license them caused a lot of work for the PCO and its principal, Chief Inspector Arthur Bassom. In 1927, to cope with this change the PCO moved to a new Metropolitan Police building in Lambeth Road, where facilities for inspecting cabs were provided. Eventually, the number of passing stations was reduced to just four, including Lambeth Road.

Over the years, the Lambeth Road premises, which had been designed to accommodate several other Metropolitan Police's administrative departments, was becoming overcrowded, so it was decided to move some of these departments out and construct a new building on the site. One of those scheduled for relocation was the PCO, which was moved to purpose-built premises in Penton Street, Islington, and these opened in 1965.

In 1985, responsibility for the PCO was transferred from the Home Office (which until 2000, had responsibility for the Metropolitan Police) to the Department of Transport. In 2000, it was transferred once more to a new body, Transport for London, which itself was part of another new body, the Greater London Authority (GLA). From that year, the PCO also took responsibility for licensing London's private-hire trade, and in 2010, the PCO was moved to new premises in Southwark Bridge Road and renamed London Taxis and Private Hire (TPH).

Appendix 2

Technical specifications

Austin FX4 and FL2, 1958 to 1971

ENGINE
Austin diesel, 4-cylinder, ohv
Bore x stroke: 3.25in (82.55mm) x 4in (101.6mm)
Cubic capacity: 132.7cu in (2,178cc)
Max bhp: 55 @ 3,500rpm
Max torque: 89lb ft @ 2,800rpm
Compression ratio: 20:1

Austin petrol, 4-cylinder, ohv
Bore x stroke: 3.125in (79.44mm) x 4.375in (111mm)
Cubic capacity: 134.1cu in (2,199cc)
Max bhp: 55.9 @ 3,750rpm
Max torque: 112lb ft @ 2,000rpm
Compression ratio: 7.5:1

TRANSMISSION
Automatic: Borg-Warner DG150/DG15M 3-speed,
later Borg-Warner BW35 3-speed
Manual: (from 1961) 4-speed synchromesh on 2nd,
3rd and top gears. Ratios: first, 4.05:1; second,
2.35:1; third, 1.37:1; top, 1:1; reverse, 5.168:1
Clutch, diesel model: coil spring, 10in (254mm)
single dry plate
Clutch, petrol model: coil spring, 9in (229mm)
single dry plate

REAR AXLE
Hypoid, 4.8:1 final drive (Early FL2: 5.125:1) three-
quarter floating

BRAKES
Four-wheel hydraulic, dual circuit with separate
master cylinders. 11in drums all round, twin leading
shoe on front. Mechanical handbrake on rear wheels

SUSPENSION
Independent with coil springs and lever arm shock
absorbers on front, semi-elliptical leaf springs with
lever arm shock absorbers on rear

ELECTRICAL
12V positive earth with dynamo

DIMENSIONS
Overall length: 14ft 11 7/16in (4.56m)
Overall height: 5ft 8 11/16in (1.74m)
Overall width: 5ft 8 5/8in (1.74m)
Wheelbase: 9ft 2 5/8in (2.81m)
Track, front: 4ft 8in (1.42m)
Track, rear: 4ft 8in (1.42m)
Turning circle: 25ft (7.62m)

Austin FX4 and FL2, 1971 to 1982 (including Carbodies FX4)

ENGINE
Austin diesel, 4-cylinder, ohv
Bore x stroke: 3.5in (88.9mm) x 4in (101.6mm)
Cubic capacity: 153.7cu in (2,520cc)
Max bhp: 63 @ 3,500rpm
Max torque: 109lb ft @ 2,000rpm
Compression ratio: 20.5:1

TRANSMISSION
Automatic: Borg-Warner BW35 3-speed.
(Borg-Warner BW365 from 1978)
Manual: 4-speed synchromesh on 2nd, 3rd and top
gears. Ratios: first, 4.05:1; second, 2.35:1; third,
1.37:1; top, 1:1; reverse, 5.168:1
Clutch, diesel model: hydraulically operated, coil
spring, 10in (254mm) single dry plate
Clutch, petrol model: coil spring, 9in (229mm)
single dry plate

REAR AXLE
Hypoid, 3.909:1 final drive, three-quarter floating

BRAKES
Four-wheel hydraulic, dual circuit with separate
master cylinders. 11in drums all round, twin leading
shoe on front. Mechanical handbrake on rear wheels

SUSPENSION
Independent with coil springs and lever arm shock
absorbers on front, semi-elliptical leaf springs with
lever arm shock absorbers on rear

ELECTRICAL
Type 12V negative earth with alternator

DIMENSIONS
Overall length: 14ft 11 7/16in (4.56m) (15ft 1/2in
[4.58m] from 1977)
Overall height: 5ft 8 11/16in (1.74m)
Overall width: 5ft 8 5/8in (1.74m)
Wheelbase: 9ft 2 5/8in (2.81m)
Track, front: 4ft 8in (1.42m)
Track, rear: 4ft 8in (1.42m)
Turning circle: 25ft (7.62m)

Carbodies FX4R and FL2R London Limousine and Austin FX4Q, 1982 to 1985

ENGINE

FX4R and FL2 London Limousine
Land Rover diesel, 4-cylinder ohv
Bore x stroke: 3.552in (90.47mm) x 3.4in (88.9mm)
Cubic capacity: 139cu in (2,286cc)
Max bhp: 62 @ 4,000rpm
Max torque: 103lb ft @ 1,800rpm
Compression ratio: 23:1

Land Rover petrol, 4-cylinder ohv
Bore x stroke: 3.552in (90.47mm) x 3.4in (88.9mm)
Cubic capacity: 139cu in (2,286cc)
Max bhp: 77 @ 4,250rpm
Max torque: 124lb ft @ 2,500rpm
Compression ratio: 7:1

FX4Q
Kalaskai diesel, 4-cylinder, ohv
Bore x stroke: 3.5in (88.9mm) x 4in (101.6mm)
Cubic capacity: 153.7cu in (2,520cc)
Max bhp: 63 @ 3,500rpm
Max torque: 109lb ft @ 2,000rpm
Compression ratio: 20.5:1

TRANSMISSION

FX4R and FL2 London Limousine
Automatic: Borg-Warner BW66 three-speed with torque converter

Manual: 5-speed synchromesh. Ratios: first, 3.592:1; second, 2.246:1; third, 1.415:1; fourth, 1:1; top, 0.821:1; reverse, 3.657:1
Clutch: hydraulically operated, diaphragm spring, 240mm (9.5in) single dry plate

FX4Q
Automatic: Borg-Warner BW66 3-speed
Manual: N/A

REAR AXLE
Hypoid, 3.909:1 final drive, three-quarter floating

BRAKES
Four-wheel hydraulic, dual circuit with separate master cylinders, full servo-assistance. 11in drums all round, twin leading shoe on front. Mechanical handbrake on rear wheels

SUSPENSION
Independent with coil springs and lever arm shock absorbers on front, semi-elliptical leaf springs with lever arm shock absorbers on rear

ELECTRICAL
Type 12V negative earth with alternator

DIMENSIONS
Overall length: 15ft 1/2in (4.58m)
Overall height: 5ft 8 11/16in (1.74m)
Overall width: 5ft 8 5/8in (1.74m)
Wheelbase: 9ft 2 5/8in (2.81m)
Track, front: 4ft 8in (1.42m)
Track, rear: 4ft 8in (1.42m)
Turning circle: 25ft (7.62m)

London Coach and London Sterling, 1985 to 1987

ENGINE
Ford petrol, 4-cylinder, sohc
Bore x stroke: 96mm (3.781in) x 79.5mm (3.126in)
Cubic capacity: 2,302cc (140.477cu in)
Max power 88bhp @ 4,800rpm
Max torque 118lb ft @ 2,800rpm
Compression ratio 9:1

TRANSMISSION
Ford C3 3-speed automatic

REAR AXLE
Hypoid, 3.909:1 final drive, three-quarter floating

BRAKES
Four-wheel hydraulic, dual circuit with separate master cylinders, full servo-assistance. 11in drums all round, twin leading shoe on front. Mechanical handbrake on rear wheels

SUSPENSION
Independent with coil springs and lever arm shock absorbers on front, semi-elliptical leaf springs with lever arm shock absorbers on rear

ELECTRICAL
Type 12V negative earth with alternator

DIMENSIONS
As per FX4R

Carbodies FX4S and FX4S-Plus, 1985 to 1989

ENGINE
Land Rover diesel, 4-cylinder, ohv
Bore x stroke: 3.562in (90.47mm) x 3.819in (97mm)
Cubic capacity 2,495cc
Max bhp: 69.6 @ 4,000rpm
Max torque: 115lb ft @ 1,800rpm
Compression ratio: 21:1

TRANSMISSION
Automatic, both models: Borg-Warner BW40
3-speed with torque converter and built-in oil cooler

Manual, both models: 5-speed synchromesh.
Ratios: first, 3.592:1; second, 2.246:1; third, 1.415:1; fourth, 1:1; top, 0.821:1; reverse, 3.657:1
Clutch: hydraulically operated, diaphragm spring, 240mm (9.5in) single dry plate

REAR AXLE
Hypoid, 3.909:1 final drive, three-quarter floating

BRAKES
Four-wheel hydraulic, twin leading shoe on front.
Dual circuit with tandem master cylinder.
11in drums all round, full servo-assistance.
Mechanical handbrake on rear wheels

SUSPENSION
FX4S
Independent with coil springs and lever arm shock absorbers on front, semi-elliptical leaf springs with lever arm shock absorbers on rear
FX4S-Plus
Independent with coil springs and lever arm shock absorbers on front, semi-elliptical Literide composite leaf springs with telescopic shock absorbers on rear

ELECTRICAL
12V negative earth with alternator

DIMENSIONS
As per FX4R

LTI Fairway, 1989 to 1992 and Fairway Driver, 1992 to 1997

ENGINE
Nissan diesel, 4-cylinder, ohv
Bore x stroke: 96mm x 92mm
Cubic capacity: 2,663cc
Max power: 63.5kw @ 4,300rpm
Max torque: 175Nm @ 2,200rpm
Compression ratio 21.8:1

TRANSMISSION
Automatic: Nissan 4-speed with oil cooler integral with radiator. Ratios: first, 2.842:1; second, 1.542:1; third, 1.00:1; fourth, 0.686:1; reverse, 2.40:1
Manual: Nissan 5-speed synchromesh. Ratios: first, 3.592:1; second, 2.246:1; third, 1.415:1; fourth, 1:1; top, 0.821:1; reverse, 3.657:1
Clutch: hydraulically operated, diaphragm spring, 240mm (9.5in) single dry plate

REAR AXLE
Hypoid, 3.909:1 final drive, three-quarter floating

BRAKES
Fairway
Four-wheel hydraulic, twin leading shoe on front.
Dual circuit with tandem master cylinder.
11in drums all round, full servo-assistance.
Mechanical handbrake on rear wheels
Fairway Driver
Front: ventilated discs with four-pot callipers.
Rear: 10in drums, self-adjusting. Cable handbrake on rear wheels

SUSPENSION
Fairway
Independent with coil springs and lever arm shock absorbers on front, semi-elliptical glassfibre leaf springs with telescopic shock absorbers on rear
Fairway Driver
Front, fully independent with double wishbones with coil springs and telescopic shock absorbers.
Rear, semi-elliptical single leaf springs with helper springs. (Earliest models – Literide composite leaf springs) with telescopic shock absorbers on rear

ELECTRICAL
Type 12V negative earth with alternator

DIMENSIONS
As per FX4R

Appendix 3

Parts availability

At the time of writing, most spares are available for all models of FX4, from the very earliest to the last Fairway 95. However, because the supply of exclusive FX4 parts is good, very little remanufacturing is taking place and spares will run short eventually, unless such parts that are unavailable are remanufactured.

Because the number of FX4s made was low in comparison with many other motor vehicles, the commercial viability of remanufacturing is not as good as it might be. Some components are common with other British vehicles, such as the tail light assembly, the instruments, the front suspension and the Land Rover engines, so it may be feasible in the future to remanufacture some obsolete parts at an economical price.

United Kingdom

Vintage Taxi Spares
The largest supply of spares for all models of FX4 taxi.
Online catalogue: www.vintagetaxispares.com
Email: parts@vintagetaxispares.com

London Taxi Exports
'Europe's largest exporter of British taxis, replacement parts and accessories'
Hope Farm
Cobblers Lane
Ridgmont
Bedfordshire
MK43 0XN
Tel.: 44 1 525 288 555
Fax: 44 1 525 288 647
E-mail: taxi@londontaxiexports.co.uk
Website: www.londontaxiexports.co.uk

USA

Kip Motor Company
Parts, service and restoration for uncommon antique British vehicles, including FX4 taxis.
2127 Crown Road
Dallas
Texas 75229
USA
Toll-free US order line: (888) 243-0440
Canada and international: (972) 243-0440
Fax: (972) 243-2387
E-mail: info@kipmotor.com
Website: www.kipmotor.com

Clubs

London Vintage Taxi Association
A worldwide club, based in the UK, catering for enthusiasts of all types of retired London taxi. Membership enquiries for UK and the rest of the world, outside the Americas:

Membership Secretary
51 Ferndale Crescent
Cowley
Uxbridge
Middlesex
UB8 2AY
Website: www.lvta.co.uk

LVTA American Section Secretary
John Freeston
PO Box 445
Windham
New Hampshire NH 03087
USA

Index